ROBERT CAVELIER, SIEUR DE LA SALLE.

THE WORLD'S GREAT EXPLORERS

René-Robert Cavelier Sieur de La Salle

By Jim Hargrove

C 1386

CHILDRENS PRESS®

CHICAGO

LaSalle's home in the vicinity of Montreal, Canada

Project Editor: Ann Heinrichs
Designer: Lindaanne Donohoe
Typsetter: Compositors Corporation
Engraver: Liberty Photoengraving

**Library of Congress
Cataloging-in-Publication Data**
Hargrove, Jim.
    René-Robert Cavelier, sieur de La Salle
/ by Jim Hargrove.
        p.   cm. — (The World's great
explorers)
    Includes bibliographical references.
    Summary: A biography of the
seventeenth-century French explorer
who, among other exploits, led the first
European expedition to track the
Mississippi River to the Gulf of Mexico.
    ISBN 0-516-03054-X
    1. La Salle, Robert Cavelier, sieur de,
1643-1687—Juvenile literature. 2.
Explorers—America—Biography—
Juvenile literature. 3. Explorers—
France—Biography—Juvenile literature.
4. Mississippi River—Discovery and
exploration—Juvenile literature. [1. La
Salle, Robert Cavelier, sieur de,
1643-1687. 2. Explorers. 3. Mississippi
River—Discovery and exploration.]
I. Title. II. Series.
F1030.5.H37 1990
917.704′1′092—dc20
[B]
[92]   89-25442
                                                CIP
                                                   AC

Evening light on the Mississippi River as viewed from Louis Point in Mississippi Palisades State Park, Carroll County, Illinois

Table of Contents

Chapter 1
The Mighty Mississippi

The Algonquin Indians called it the *Missi Sippi,* which means "Father of Waters." It is easy to see why they considered this river so special. On the vast North American continent, there was—and still is—nothing else quite like the mighty Mississippi.

More than 250 other rivers flow into the waters of the Mississippi. Some of them, such as the Missouri, Ohio, Arkansas, and Red, are enormous rivers themselves. The Father of Waters and its hundreds of children stretch as far north as Canada, west to the Rocky Mountains, east to the Appalachians, and southward to the Gulf of Mexico. Rainwater from thirty-one different U.S. states eventually finds its way into the Mississippi.

The American author Mark Twain became famous writing about the great river. Two of his best known characters, Tom Sawyer and Huckleberry Finn, shared grand adventures along the Mississippi. Mark Twain understood the river better than almost anyone. He grew up in a little Missouri town nestled along its banks. When he was a young man, he served as a Mississippi riverboat captain for several years.

MARK TWAIN
PILOT
LIFE
COPYRIGHT 1905

AMERICAN HUMOR

ALBERT LEVERING

Caricature of Mark Twain, from a 1905 magazine cover

"Considering the Missouri its main branch," he wrote in *Life on the Mississippi,* "it is the longest river in the world—four thousand three hundred miles. It seems safe to say that it is also the crookedest river in the world, since in one part of its journey it uses up one thousand three hundred miles to cover the same ground that the crow would fly over in six hundred and seventy-five. It discharges three times as much water as the St. Lawrence, twenty-five times as much as the Rhine, and three hundred and thirty-eight times as much as the Thames. . . . The area of its drainage basin is as great as the combined areas of England, Wales, Scotland, Ireland, France, Spain, Portugal, Germany, Austria, Italy, and Turkey."

Today's accurate measurements show that Mark Twain went a bit too far in describing his beloved river. Both the Nile River in Africa and the Amazon River in South America are slightly longer than the Mississippi. Still, no one can deny the majesty and the historical importance of the mighty Mississippi River.

In 1850, when Mark Twain was a teenager, the Mississippi was a great highway in America's heartland. Riverboats paddled downstream carrying corn, wheat, lumber, tobacco, and furs. From ports such as New Orleans, ships hauled cotton, sugar, molasses, and whiskey.

Even today, in an age of airplanes, trains, and automobiles, the Mississippi remains a great commercial highway. Groups of barges, each bigger than a football field, are moved up and down the river by diesel-powered towboats. Just three of these powerful barges can move more cargo than all the steamboats on the Mississippi did in 1850. In earlier times, however, the Mississippi River flowed more quietly.

A plantation along the Mississippi River in the mid-1800s

Indians hollowing out a log to make a dugout canoe

For centuries before European explorers arrived, the river was in Indian country. Among the tribes that settled along its banks were the Sioux, Fox, Potawatomie, Kickapoo, Iowa, Illinois, Miami, Chickasaw, Otoe, and Quapaw.

In the north, where white birch trees were plentiful, the Indians made swift, lightweight canoes covered with birch bark. European explorers marveled at these canoes and soon copied their construction. In the south, where birch trees were rare, the Indians made much heavier canoes, called dugouts. Dugout canoes were made by hollowing out huge logs with fire and stone tools.

There may well have been great explorers among the Indian tribes of early America. Some may have traveled on the Father of Waters for great distances. But without written histories of their adventures, we will probably never learn about them. We know much, however, about the first European explorer to travel the length of the great river.

He was a French explorer who lived more than three centuries ago. His name was René-Robert Cavelier, Sieur de La Salle. In its shortest form, we know his name as Robert La Salle.

In December 1681, La Salle led an expedition of French explorers and American Indians down the Illinois River. That river, La Salle knew, flowed directly into the Mississippi. Although they had birch-bark canoes, the explorers were walking. It was the dead of winter, and the Illinois River was frozen. The men pulled their canoes on sleds across the ice and snow. La Salle was leading a great voyage that he knew would cover thousands of miles. The group had to travel year-round, not just during the warm months of the year.

A band of fur traders journeying upstream in the Canadian wilderness; from a print dated 1865

An eighteenth-century map of North America by German mapmaker Johannes Homann

La Salle and his followers had already completed a long trip just to reach the Illinois River. They had come from French settlements far to the northeast, in present-day Canada. During the difficult journey, some of La Salle's men had given up and refused to go on. Only twenty-three Frenchmen now remained in the party of explorers. Traveling with them were thirty-one American Indians, including ten women and three children.

After several days of difficult travel on the ice-bound river, the expedition reached a place where the river widened and formed a lake. Here, the ice finally thawed and broke up. Although the weather was still cold, the explorers could use their canoes to make travel easier.

On February 6, 1682, La Salle and some of his followers reached the Mississippi River. Huge cakes of ice were floating dangerously down the river, forcing them to make camp for a while. The jagged ice could rip apart even the best-made canoe. The halt also allowed the Indians, who had followed on foot, to catch up to the rest of the expedition.

It was not the first time La Salle had seen the Father of Waters. But as he rested he undoubtedly thought about the adventure that lay ahead. He had not one but two grand plans.

The first was to follow the great river wherever it led. No other European explorer had managed to trace it all the way to its end. His second plan was to build permanent forts along the river, to be guarded by French soldiers. Then France could control the heartland of the New World. If both plans had succeeded, most of the United States might have become a French colony—and this book might have been written in French.

A 1684 map of New France, Louisiana, and other North American lands

Chapter 2
From the
Old World to the New

La Salle's full name was René-Robert Cavelier, Sieur de La Salle. He was born in 1643, near the city of Rouen, France. If La Salle were alive today, he might still recognize many familiar sights in the city of his birth. Much of Rouen appears the same now as it did so long ago.

Rouen still lies on the north bank of the Seine River, about 70 miles (113 kilometers) northwest of Paris. Visitors today enjoy Rouen's "old town," the central section of the city. There they stroll through streets that have been carefully preserved to appear hundreds of years old. In central Rouen, automobiles are banned. Many of the streets are narrow. Some are still paved with cobblestones, just as they were when Robert was born.

Many of the homes lining the narrow avenues are truly old. Others, destroyed during World War II, have been rebuilt to appear old. Most are made from wooden beams covered with stucco, a building material similar to cement. As a young boy, Robert surely saw many of the same old buildings that travelers view today when they visit Rouen.

Near the Seine River in Rouen, the elaborate spires of old cathedrals and church buildings rise toward the heavens. Records discovered in the 1800s show that the infant Robert was baptized in Rouen's Roman Catholic church on November 22, 1643. His name on the baptismal record was simply Robert Cavelier.

Robert came from a large, wealthy family. Both his father and his uncle were prosperous businessmen. His father's name was Jean Cavelier and his mother was named Catherine. Robert had many other relatives, including an older brother also named Jean. Members of the large Cavelier family spread over much of France.

Near Rouen, Robert's father owned a huge estate called La Salle. Robert was probably born on this estate. So that other relatives would know exactly who he was, the words "Sieur de La Salle" were added to Robert's name. This is French for "the gentleman from La Salle."

When he was a young boy, Robert began attending school at a church in Rouen. His school was run by Jesuits, Catholic priests of a religious order called the Society of Jesus. Jesuits were dedicated to teaching. Their students often received the finest instruction available in seventeenth-century Europe.

Robert must have been excited by school lessons describing the great discoveries of Christopher Columbus and other explorers. Even before Robert was born, a few Europeans had already crossed the Atlantic Ocean in sailboats to settle in North America. Because they had been discovered so recently, the Americas were called the New World.

After the voyages of Columbus, Spaniards explored the land along the southern coast of what is now the United States. Some of these men were Ponce de León, Francisco de Coronado, and Alvar Nuñez Cabeza de

Spanish explorer Juan Ponce de León, who discovered Florida

Hernando de Soto

Vaca. On May 8, 1541, a Spanish army led by Hernando de Soto traveled to what is today the northern part of the state of Mississippi. There the soldiers found an enormous river, bigger than any in Europe. They called it the *Rio Grande,* meaning "great river." Probably for the first time, European explorers had found a southern stretch of the Father of Waters.

Soon disease and Indian battles took the lives of De Soto and many of his soldiers. The survivors built small sailboats, rafts, and canoes to escape the hostile tribes by sailing down the great river. Two weeks later they reached the Gulf of Mexico, whose waters are part of the Atlantic Ocean.

Spaniards tried to establish a few settlements near the mouth of the river, but none did well. Before long, they lost interest in the river. In 1565, Spaniards established the first permanent European settlement in the United States. It was in present-day Florida, about 400 miles (645 kilometers) east of the Mississippi River.

René-Robert Cavelier, Sieur de La Salle, was born 102 years after De Soto discovered the river he called the *Rio Grande*. However, it is not clear how much his Jesuit teachers knew about Spanish explorations. Since the time of Columbus, Spain had tried to keep its New World discoveries secret. But the Jesuits did know of French explorations in lands far to the north.

French explorers, more than any other Europeans, were claiming land in what is now southeastern Canada. In 1497 John Cabot, an Italian sailing for England, was the first European known to have reached Canada. But French explorers, such as Jacques Cartier, followed soon afterwards. Cartier is best remembered as the man who discovered the St. Lawrence River. Today, part of that river forms the boundary between the United States and Canada.

Jacques Cartier

In 1535, Jacques Cartier led an expedition of ten ships up the St. Lawrence River. Eventually they were stopped by the dangerous rapids near present-day Montreal. Cartier tried to establish a colony in Canada, which he called New France. His settlers, however, could not survive in the wilderness and eventually returned to Europe. Despite Cartier's early failure, the river he discovered soon became a highway for French explorers in North America.

Explorers soon discovered the importance of the St. Lawrence River. They found that it linked the Atlantic Ocean with the five Great Lakes of the North American

Cartier on the summit of Mont Real, now Montreal

interior. Together the Great Lakes make up the largest body of fresh water in the world.

The interior of the North American continent was vast and wild. Thus, the earliest Spanish and English settlers stayed close to the seacoast. But the French used the wide St. Lawrence River as a watery highway for moving their boats and canoes deep into the continent. By the early 1600s, before Robert was even born, wandering Frenchmen had developed a fur trade with Indians along the St. Lawrence.

Fur traders bartering with Indians for furs

Fur trading began soon after the first Frenchmen arrived in the New World. French fishermen sailed to the coast of Nova Scotia (now a part of Canada) in 1504, only twelve years after Christopher Columbus first reached the New World. These early French explorers soon lost interest in fishing. They discovered that animals like beaver, fox, rabbit, and deer were plentiful in the New World. The furs of these animals could be made into coats, hats, and other warm clothing. Fur pelts, especially from the beaver, were prized in Europe and brought many traders great wealth.

The French fishermen quickly discovered that Indians living near the St. Lawrence were willing to trade animal furs for little pieces of metal and small amounts of gunpowder. The Europeans could make a fortune trading almost worthless trinkets for the valuable furs. Many of the people who moved from France to settle along the St. Lawrence River were, or soon became, fur traders. From the Indian word *kanata,* meaning "village," the area soon became known in French as *Le Canada.*

In 1608, a French explorer named Samuel de Champlain built a trading post, called Quebec, along the St. Lawrence. The Quebec post was more than 300 miles (484 kilometers) inland from the Atlantic. Champlain later explored Lake Huron and Lake Ontario, two of the enormous Great Lakes.

Samuel de Champlain

A drawing of the 1609 battle at Ticonderoga, showing the first use of firearms in Indian tribal warfare

Below: French missionary praying for the Indians

Champlain made friends with the Algonquin and Huron Indians in the area and traded with them for furs. He persuaded them to allow Catholic missionaries to live among them and teach them about Christianity. He also helped these Indians battle their powerful enemies, the Iroquois. In a 1609 war, Champlain helped the Algonquins and Hurons defeat the Iroquois. After that the Iroquois became enemies of the French, too.

In 1638, a French fur trader named Jean Nicolet paddled a canoe from the St. Lawrence all the way to Lake Michigan, one of the two westernmost Great Lakes. On Lake Michigan, Nicolet journeyed as far south as the inlet known today as Green Bay, Wisconsin. After that remarkable voyage, however, he could go no farther. Like many explorers, Nicolet was searching for a water route to the Pacific Ocean and China. But he found no such route beyond Lake Michigan.

Nicolet did not know it, but he was an easy three-day walk from the Wisconsin River, which leads to the Mississippi. Some later explorers thought that the great Mississippi might lead to the Pacific Ocean. Although Nicolet may have heard stories from Indians about a vast river to the west, he decided to return to the familiar St. Lawrence.

In 1642, one year before Robert was born, another French settlement was started in New France. The little town, built on an island in the St. Lawrence, was called Montreal. It is located just where the famous Canadian city is found today, about 80 miles (130 kilometers) north of present-day New York state.

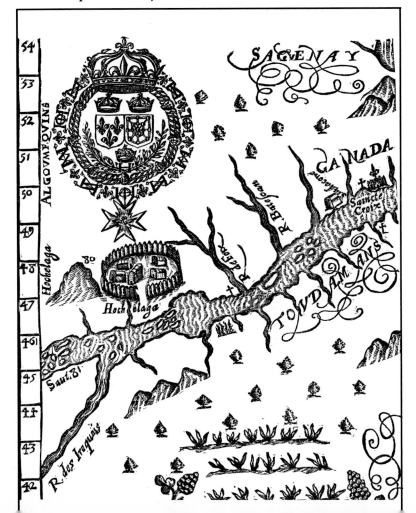

Lescarbot's 1609 map of the site of Montreal, formerly the Indian town of Hochelaga. Lescarbot was not aware at the time that Montreal was an island in the St. Lawrence River.

Across the Atlantic Ocean in France, Robert La Salle heard of these explorations with great interest. By the time Robert was in school, however, the French had stopped all their westward explorations in North America. New France was at war with the Iroquois Indians. The Iroquois were a powerful league of five, and later six, Indian nations. For year after brutal year, the little settlements of New France were barely able to survive.

Even though the classes at the Jesuit school were hard, Robert was an excellent student. The priests soon found that he was especially skilled at mathematics. They also regarded his good behavior as a fine example for the other students. Robert must have studied hard in all his courses, but he may have been most interested in news from the New World. Soon he had even more reason to be fascinated by the faraway land.

While Robert was still in school, his older brother, Jean, joined a religious order called the Sulpicians. Soon afterward, the new Abbé Jean Cavelier sailed away to Montreal to be a missionary. This surely increased Robert's desire to see the New World for himself.

Instead, he continued his education at the Jesuit school in Rouen. He grew tall and thin, with long black hair that reached his shoulders. Although his education was preparing him to become a Jesuit priest, he gradually lost interest in the religious life.

Work at the Jesuit school was hard, and the hours of each day were filled with study, prayer, and meditation. Robert's increasing desire for adventure began to clash with the quiet life-style of the Jesuits. Sometime around his twenty-second birthday, Robert asked his superiors to send him to the New World as a missionary. They refused, saying he had to wait until he took his final vows at age twenty-five.

Totem or tribe-mark of the nations of the Iroquois confederacy

Drawing of the Gothic cathedral in Rouen, France, by J. M. W. Turner

Impatient, Robert left the school. He remained a loyal Catholic all his life, but he held no great affection for the Jesuit order. His connection with the Jesuits also caused him financial problems. Under French law, a Jesuit, even a former Jesuit novice like Robert, could not inherit any of his family's fortune. As far as money was concerned, Robert had dim prospects for the future.

In the year 1665, tragedy struck his family and much of Europe. Off and on since the middle 1300s, a mysterious disease called the plague had swept through Europe and other parts of the world. Between 1346 and 1352, about twenty-five million people died from the disease in Europe alone.

Victims of the plague were buried in mass graves.

Three centuries later, when Robert was a young man, the plague broke out once again in Europe. It was especially severe in England. In the capital city of London, at least 68,000 people died from the plague in 1665. Outbreaks in other European cities were less severe but no less frightening.

"This disease is making us more cruel to one another than we are to dogs," an Englishman wrote in 1665. An Italian wrote that the plague had killed all five of his children, and he had to bury them with his own hands.

Robert's father died in 1665, when the new outbreak of the plague was at its worst. The young Frenchman could not inherit any of his father's fortune, but his family was able to give him a tiny allowance. He soon put the money to good use.

The following year, 1666, twenty-two-year-old Robert decided to leave the Old World for the new. He bought a ticket on a ship sailing across the Atlantic Ocean and a few weeks later entered the wide mouth of the St. Lawrence River.

After years of anticipation, Robert was about to see the New World. He may already have made up his mind to see more of it than anyone else in his time.

Robert La Salle as a young man

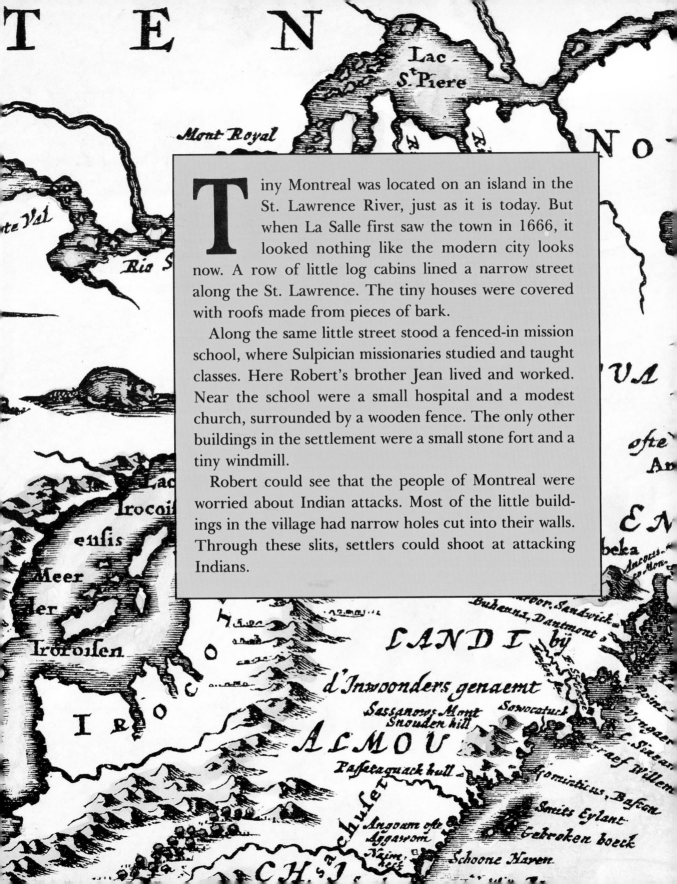

Tiny Montreal was located on an island in the St. Lawrence River, just as it is today. But when La Salle first saw the town in 1666, it looked nothing like the modern city looks now. A row of little log cabins lined a narrow street along the St. Lawrence. The tiny houses were covered with roofs made from pieces of bark.

Along the same little street stood a fenced-in mission school, where Sulpician missionaries studied and taught classes. Here Robert's brother Jean lived and worked. Near the school were a small hospital and a modest church, surrounded by a wooden fence. The only other buildings in the settlement were a small stone fort and a tiny windmill.

Robert could see that the people of Montreal were worried about Indian attacks. Most of the little buildings in the village had narrow holes cut into their walls. Through these slits, settlers could shoot at attacking Indians.

Above: Iroquois warrior
Below: An Indian encampment along the St. Lawrence River

Montreal was the westernmost of all the French settlements in North America. It was also the most difficult to protect. For more than twenty years—most of La Salle's young life—French pioneers in Canada had fought fierce battles with the Iroquois Indians.

In 1666, the year Robert arrived in Montreal, French soldiers defeated the Iroquois Indians in a battle south of the St. Lawrence. Iroquois leaders then signed a peace treaty with the French. For the first time in many years, French settlers in Canada were free to pursue their most important activities—farming and fur trading.

For a while, La Salle joined the other pioneers settling in and near Montreal. Probably with the help of his brother Jean, he purchased from the Sulpicians a large tract of land near the southern end of Montreal island. On his new property, Robert cut down some trees to make a little clearing. There he built a fort surrounded by a sturdy log fence and set up a trading post.

Robert's land was only a few miles south of the Montreal settlement, but the thick woods made it difficult to travel there. It took several hours to hike from the settlement to his property. Nevertheless, he soon convinced other colonists to move there too. He rented small tracts of land to them at the southern end of the island.

The missionaries were happy to see people settling down in other places on the island. These farmers, hunters, trappers, and fur traders would be able to help defend the entire island if there were trouble with the Indians again.

As soon as La Salle finished building his little community, he began exploring the area around him. He traveled far from Montreal, meeting Indians from many different tribes. On these travels he made careful studies of the Indians' languages. Within a few years, it is said, he mastered the Iroquois language and could speak fairly well in seven or eight other Indian tongues.

A Canadian trapper

Among the Iroquois, former enemies of the French settlers, was the Seneca tribe. One day in 1668, a group of Seneca warriors visited Robert at his farm. Staying for much of the long Canadian winter, the visitors told him about a great river to the south. The Seneca Indians called the river the Ohio, meaning "beautiful water." By following the Ohio in a canoe for eight or nine months, they said, one could reach the sea.

The Ohio River at Cave-in-Rock State Park, Illinois

Historians believe that "Ohio" may have been the name the Seneca Indians used for the Mississippi River. However, it is also possible that they were referring to the modern Ohio River we know today.

The Senecas' information astonished Robert La Salle. Here was the first news of a river deep in the North American heartland that led to an ocean. But which ocean did the Indians mean? La Salle hoped that the river led to what Frenchmen of his time called the Vermilion Sea. Today we know this "sea" was the Gulf of California, which flows into the Pacific Ocean.

Like many other seventeenth-century explorers, La Salle hoped to find a water route through North America to the Pacific Ocean and China. This quest may sound odd to us today. Yet it is easy to understand if we remember what spurred the discovery of the New World. When Christopher Columbus landed in the New World, he was really searching for China. Many of the explorers who followed him were also looking for a water route to the Orient. The continents of North and South America, however, stood in the way. Perhaps, La Salle thought, he could discover the course that so many others had failed to find.

Instead of starting on a long voyage right away, La Salle decided to plan his travels carefully. He thought it would be best to describe his plans to the French governor of Canada. Governor Courcelle lived in Quebec, about 170 miles (274 kilometers) down the St. Lawrence River from Montreal.

With four other men, Robert traveled to Quebec in the late spring or early summer of 1669. Like other French pioneers in Canada, the men traveled in birch-bark canoes. These little boats were made in much the same way as the canoes built by Indians who lived along the St. Lawrence.

From cedar trees, which resist rot, the Frenchmen cut long, narrow boards. These would form the frames. When placed in boiling water, the boards became soft enough to bend into the rough shape of the boat. The boards were then tied together with leather ropes.

The bark of the white birch tree made an ideal skin for the lightweight canoes. It was thin and flexible but very strong. In spring and fall, when sap was rising in the trees, the bark could be peeled away easily from the trunk. While still moist, large pieces of bark were sewn to the cedar framework of the canoe. As it dried, the bark became very tough. Leaks were plugged with the gummy resin of spruce trees.

A. Le Fort
B. les Recollets
C. La plate forme
D. Les Jesuites
E. La Cathedralle
F. Le Seminaire
G. l'Hostel Dieu
H. L'évéché
I. La Redoute
K. Le magazin a poudre

A drawing of the city of Quebec as it appeared in 1664

For traveling on wide rivers like the St. Lawrence, or on narrow streams of the Canadian backwoods, the birch-bark canoe had no equal. Small ones were light enough for one man to carry easily around rapids and other obstacles. They could also be built large enough to carry more than a dozen passengers.

Traveling in their swift canoes, Robert La Salle and his followers quickly reached Quebec. There, Governor Courcelle listened as Robert explained his plan to explore the North American interior. He surely told the story of the great river the Senecas called the Ohio. He probably admitted that he did not know which ocean the river fed. Whether it flowed into the Pacific or the Gulf of Mexico, it could be of great use to the people of New France.

If it led to the Pacific, as La Salle hoped, the river would provide the long-sought water route to China. Even if it flowed into the Gulf of Mexico, it could be used as a smooth highway through the American wilderness to the French island of Martinique. This island belonged to a group of Caribbean islands called the West Indies. Martinique was famous for producing sugar, tobacco, and rum, all in short supply in Canada.

Governor Courcelle gave his blessing to La Salle's expedition. Unfortunately, the governor added, Robert would have to pay for the voyage himself. Courcelle prepared legal papers authorizing the voyage that same year. However, he could offer Robert no money to help with expenses.

Cut off from his wealthy family's inheritance, La Salle had little money of his own. When he returned to Montreal island, he decided to raise money for the trip by selling his land. The missionaries realized that La Salle was intent on exploring, so they agreed to buy back part of his land. By refusing to buy all of it, they could perhaps keep him tied to his property.

La Salle, however, had other plans. He promptly sold what was left of his land to an ironworker named Jean Milot. With the money he made, he bought four canoes and all the supplies needed for the long voyage. He also hired fourteen men to accompany him. Though usually a quiet man, La Salle talked excitedly about his exploration plans. If he could find the "Ohio," perhaps it would lead through North America to the Pacific Ocean. Then he might even be able to open up a trade route with China.

The missionaries in Montreal, including Robert's brother Jean, hated to lose one of their most energetic settlers. They urged La Salle to join forces with a group of their own missionaries. Led by a huge priest named Dollier de Casson, these missionaries planned to explore the land west of Montreal. There they hoped to find Indians they could convert to Christianity. Seeing Jesuit missionaries as rivals, the Sulpicians wanted to outdo the Jesuits in making converts.

La Salle had other interests, but he agreed to join his expedition with Casson's. In all, twenty-four men and seven canoes took part in the journey. At long last, it seemed as if La Salle would have his dream of exploring the American interior.

Shortly before the expedition was to begin, however, serious trouble arose. During the summer of 1669, three soldiers from the French fort at Montreal murdered a Seneca chief. The soldiers were put on trial. During the trial, it was learned that three other Frenchmen had murdered a number of Oneida Indians while stealing their furs.

Both the Senecas and the Oneidas were members of the powerful Iroquois confederacy. Suddenly, it looked as if the French and the Iroquois might again go to war. Their truce had lasted only three years. A war with the Iroquois would make any voyage of discovery a suicide mission.

To make matters worse, the men who killed the Oneida Indians for their furs escaped. The trial of the French soldiers, however, continued. They were convicted and shot by a firing squad on July 6, 1669. Many Iroquois Indians watched the execution and were satisfied that justice had been done. Thus the French avoided a bloody war.

La Salle, Casson, and the other twenty-two Frenchmen in the expedition now felt it was safe to leave Montreal. With a group of Seneca Indians acting as guides, they set their canoes into the St. Lawrence River on the same day as the execution. La Salle's first voyage of exploration had begun.

La Salle visiting an Indian lead mine

Chapter 4
The Mysterious Journey

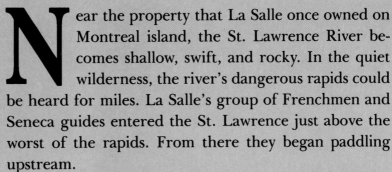

N ear the property that La Salle once owned on Montreal island, the St. Lawrence River becomes shallow, swift, and rocky. In the quiet wilderness, the river's dangerous rapids could be heard for miles. La Salle's group of Frenchmen and Seneca guides entered the St. Lawrence just above the worst of the rapids. From there they began paddling upstream.

Other than the Indians, few men in the expedition had ventured on long trips into the North American wilderness. None of the missionaries led by Father Dollier de Casson had ever tried such a difficult trek. La Salle himself, now twenty-six years old, had explored the land around Montreal. But he had never before attempted a great voyage of exploration. Nevertheless, the explorers packed plenty of corn, gunpowder, ammunition, and other supplies into their sturdy birch-bark canoes. Their spirits were high as they set out upon the St. Lawrence River.

Although La Salle kept a journal describing his explorations, it was lost over the years. Fortunately, however, a priest and mapmaker on the expedition, Father Galinée, kept a diary. His account has survived for all these years.

An Indian stripping the bark of a birch tree to make a birch-bark canoe

Among his earliest entries, Father Galinée told of his admiration for the Indian birch-bark canoe. "If God grants me the grace of returning to France," he wrote, "I shall try to carry one with me." In his diary, the priest told how the men made camp after they had finished paddling on the St. Lawrence each day.

"Your lodging is as extraordinary as your vessels," he wrote, "for, after paddling or carrying the canoes all day, you find mother earth ready to receive your wearied body. If the weather is fair, you make a fire and lie down to sleep without further trouble; but if it rains, you must peel bark from the trees, and make a shed by laying it on a frame of sticks."

"As for your food," Father Galinée continued, "it is enough to make you burn all the cookery books that ever were written; for in the woods of Canada one finds means to live well without bread, wine, salt, pepper, or spice. The ordinary food is Indian corn, or Turkey wheat as they call it in France, which is crushed between two stones and boiled, seasoning it with meat or fish, when you can get it."

For several weeks, La Salle and his party followed the St. Lawrence River. At times the going was fairly easy, even though they had to paddle against a swift current. But all too often, the men had to carry their canoes through thick forests to get around obstacles in the water. The work was often exhausting, and the surroundings strange. Before long, some of the explorers began to feel exhausted.

Travelers in the Canadian wilderness often had to portage, or carry their canoes, through the forest.

"This sort of life seemed so strange to us that we all felt the effects of it," Father Galinée wrote, "and before we were a hundred leagues [about 300 miles, or 480 kilometers] from Montreal, not one of us was free from some malady or another." At the time, no one in La Salle's party knew how far they would have to travel to follow the great, unknown river to the sea.

If he had known the truth, Father Galinée may have felt more miserable. Even if the men followed the shortest route to the river and then to the sea, the voyage ahead was still more than ten times longer than the distance they had traveled so far. For his part, Robert La Salle behaved as he would in all his voyages of discovery. He kept pushing ahead in silence, saying nothing to his companions for hours at a time.

"At last, after all our misery," Father Galinée continued, "on the second of August, we discovered Lake Ontario, like a great sea with no land beyond it." Despite the priest's words, however, Lake Ontario was hardly a discovery. Earlier French explorers had already found all five of the Great Lakes. Lake Ontario, closest of the lakes to Montreal, had been seen by a number of French explorers and missionaries, and probably by roaming fur traders as well.

After paddling their canoes along the southern shore of Lake Ontario for eight days, La Salle's party reached Irondequoit Bay, near the modern city of Rochester, New York. There, they met a band of Seneca Indians.

The Indians welcomed the Frenchmen and invited them to their village. La Salle, Galinée, and eight of the other men decided to accompany the Indians on the several-hour walk to the village. Father Dollier de Casson and the rest of the Frenchmen remained with the canoes.

When Robert and the others finally reached the village, they found it on a hill surrounded by a rough wooden fence. The Seneca town was made up of about one hundred fifty huts made of bark. The largest of all was given to the Frenchmen for resting after their travels.

While living in Montreal, La Salle had studied Iroquois languages, including that of the Seneca. He thought he understood it well. But on meeting these Senecas, he found that he could not understand a word they said. They could not understand him, either. Fortunately, a French Jesuit missionary already lived at the Indian village. The missionary's assistant was able to translate between the French and Indian tongues.

Indian settlement surrounded by wooden stakes, or palisades, for protection

Drawing of a Canadian Indian; tribe unknown

La Salle and his followers stayed as guests at the Indian village for several weeks. Soon after their arrival, the Senecas learned of the murder of an Indian chief near Montreal. Although many of them were angered by the incident, they nevertheless treated their guests well. Seneca children brought the Frenchmen fresh berries and pumpkins from the woods. Great feasts were held, the food including dog meat, an Indian delicacy, and corn cooked with fresh oil pressed from nuts and sunflower seeds.

One day, La Salle left the village on a hunting trip. While he was gone, a group of Seneca warriors returned to the village with a young Indian captured from a rival village. When Galinée saw the captive, he had an idea.

The Frenchmen needed an Indian guide who could help them find the great river they were seeking. Perhaps they could buy the young captive from the Seneca and use him as a guide. Galinée offered to do just that, but the Indians had other ideas.

"I saw the most miserable spectacle I ever beheld in my life," Galinée wrote in his diary. The unfortunate captive was tied to a stake and tortured for six hours. Then he was killed and his body was cut up and eaten by the Senecas of the village. It was a custom among some American Indian tribes to devour their enemies, but the French explorers were shocked by what they saw.

La Salle and his followers soon discovered that they were in potential danger themselves. Some of the Senecas were drinking whiskey and making threatening speeches. They suggested killing the Frenchmen in return for the murder of the Indian chief near Montreal. Before long, La Salle wisely decided that he was in danger of overstaying his welcome. With the other explorers, he returned quickly to the Lake Ontario shore.

There they rejoined Father Dollier de Casson and the others who had stayed behind to guard the canoes.

The explorers continued along the south shore of Lake Ontario. Before long, they drifted by the mouth of the Niagara River. In the distance, La Salle and the others could hear the roar of the famous Niagara Falls. Rather than enter the dangerous river, they continued moving westward along the shore of the huge lake.

At the western edge of Lake Ontario, they found a village filled with friendly Indians. Almost as soon as they arrived, they were amazed to learn that another French explorer was camped nearby. His name was Lucien Jolliet, and he had a brother named Louis Jolliet. Louis would soon play an important role in the history of the still undiscovered river to the west.

Horseshoe Falls, part of Niagara Falls, in Ontario, Canada

In the meantime, Lucien met with La Salle and the others. Unfortunately, Lucien was a friend of the Jesuit religious order. Rather than help rival Sulpician missionaries traveling with La Salle, Lucien decided to give them some bad advice.

Lucien knew that the Sulpicians were very interested in converting Indians to the Christian religion. He told the priests that there were many Indians in need of religious help around the Great Lakes to the west and north of Lake Ontario. He neglected to tell them that many Jesuit missionaries were already preaching to the Indians there.

La Salle had no interest in heading northwest. He knew that, to reach the vast river he sought, it would be best to travel along the southern shores of the Great Lakes. The Ohio River described by the Senecas lay somewhere to the south.

At this point, the party of explorers split into two groups. Father Galinée and the other Sulpicians decided to follow Father Dollier de Casson in search of converts. The missionaries began preparing for a long journey to the north. La Salle, pretending to have had enough of the dangers of the wilderness, said that he would return to Montreal. At an altar held up by canoe paddles, Father Dollier blessed La Salle and his followers and prayed for their safe return to Montreal. Then the Sulpicians began their voyage toward Lake Superior, northernmost of all the Great Lakes.

They left behind La Salle, thirteen other men, four canoes, and a share of the supplies. As soon as Father Dollier and his followers left, La Salle made a surprising announcement. They would not be returning to Montreal but would head south, searching for the Ohio River described by the Senecas.

For historians writing about Robert La Salle, it is unfortunate that Father Galinée headed north with the other Sulpicians. Although the trip allowed him to make the first accurate map of all the Great Lakes, he could no longer write about La Salle in his diary. Where La Salle traveled and what he did for the next two years is shrouded in mystery.

Francis Parkman, a nineteenth-century historian, adds even more mystery. According to Parkman, La Salle's elderly niece, Madeleine Cavelier, had La Salle's own journal in her possession as late as 1756. But sometime after that year, Parkman wrote, the journal completely vanished.

The Great Lakes region, from a French map engraved around the year 1700

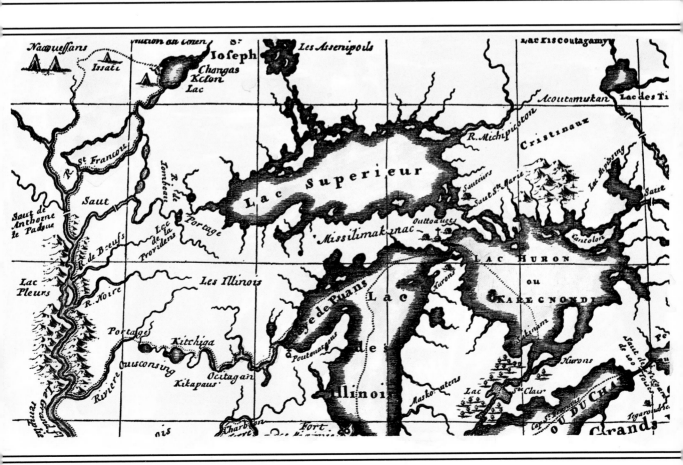

From about 1669 to 1671, La Salle also vanished from public record. It is believed that, sometime during the winter of 1669 to 1670, his men deserted him, stealing most of his supplies and leaving him alone in the frozen wilderness. Some historians think that the men headed east, hoping to surrender to English or Dutch colonists near the Atlantic coast. History offers no clear trace of them. As for La Salle, he probably survived by eating wild plants and game in the wilderness. Probably, too, he was aided by friendly Indians whose languages he could speak.

Later, after he had returned to civilization, La Salle himself had plenty of opportunities to boast about his years alone in the American wilderness. But he seldom, if ever, did. He was not a talkative man, and he almost never bragged about his deeds.

There is, however, one strange and fascinating account of his years alone in the wilds. Probably in the late 1670s or early 1680s, an article was published in France called *Histoire de Monsieur de La Salle* ("Story of the Gentleman from La Salle"). The author, whose name was not given, claimed to have met with La Salle ten or twelve times while Robert was in Paris on a visit. The anonymous author admitted never having been to America, and the story contained a few obvious errors.

Many of the facts, however, may be true. According to the article, La Salle discovered a branch of the Ohio and paddled down it until he reached the main river. This he followed until he reached dangerous rapids. Today, the Falls of the Ohio are found near the city of Louisville, Kentucky. At that point, the story continued, La Salle's men abandoned him.

According to the story, La Salle then headed northward alone, traveling on Lake Erie, Lake Huron, and

Lake Michigan, three of the Great Lakes. Moving south of Lake Michigan, he found a large river heading west, probably the Illinois River. He followed it, said the article, until he reached another large river flowing from the northwest to the southeast. Only the mighty Mississippi River itself matches that description.

History books say that Louis Jolliet, not Robert La Salle, was the first European to discover the upper Mississippi River. Could the history books be wrong? It is possible, of course, but not probable. According to people who spoke with La Salle in later years, he claimed to have discovered only the Ohio and Illinois rivers. Only one unreliable account said that he also claimed to have discovered the upper Mississippi.

Whether or not Robert La Salle was the first European explorer to reach the upper Mississippi, his greatest adventures still lay ahead on that mighty river.

French explorers Jacques Marquette and Louis Jolliet crossing the Wisconsin River with a guide

Chapter 5
Planning the
Great Adventure

Robert La Salle reappeared in Montreal sometime during the year 1671. He must have had mixed feelings about his homecoming. Some people in the village thought that, after wandering in the wilderness alone for so long, the explorer had gone a little mad. When he left his island home two years earlier, after all, he was seeking a route to the Pacific Ocean and China. He had completely failed to achieve that goal. But almost immediately, he began talking about new voyages.

Some of his Montreal neighbors began to make fun of him. They called his former property on the island *La Chine,* which means "China" in French. Today the famous stretch of white water on the St. Lawrence River near his former estate is still called the Lachine Rapids.

Although La Salle had failed to find a water route to the Pacific, he started making even bolder plans for his next expedition. Some of these plans seem ambitious even today. One can only imagine what they must have sounded like to his neighbors in Montreal.

Louis de Buade, the Count of Frontenac

By this time, Robert was almost certain that the undiscovered river flowed into the Gulf of Mexico, not the Pacific Ocean. Descriptions by Indians familiar with the Mississippi convinced him of this. He began planning not only to explore the river but to claim the land along it for New France.

La Salle shared his dreams with a man who came to Montreal from France in the summer of 1672. The new arrival's name was Louis de Buade, a nobleman with the title of Count of Frontenac. The king of France, Louis XIV, had just appointed Frontenac to the post of governor of New France.

Although many of the citizens of Montreal scoffed at his ideas, La Salle found that the new governor listened seriously. Robert told Governor Frontenac about his plans to find the Mississippi River, to travel down it to the Gulf of Mexico, and to build a series of French forts along the river's banks. The forts, Robert believed, would allow the French government to control the interior of the North American continent. This would help the French to expand their valuable fur trade.

La Salle had even bolder plans. He suggested using the lower Mississippi as a military base. From there, France could launch an army of soldiers and Indians— led by himself—against Spanish forts around the Gulf of Mexico. Then, La Salle reasoned, the French could control all of what is now the United States, except for the east coast. Sooner or later, he felt, the English and Dutch colonies there would also be ruled by the king of France.

Many people thought his ideas were crazy. La Salle had little experience as a soldier, much less as a military leader. But Governor Frontenac was impressed by at least some of the well-educated man's plans. There was, however, a major problem to overcome before La Salle could begin any of his adventures.

The Iroquois Indians were once again causing trouble throughout much of New France. Bad feelings between the native Americans and the French colonists were threatening not only La Salle's grand scheme but also the valuable fur trade.

Wisely, Governor Frontenac decided to arrange a meeting with the Iroquois to work out their differences. He sent La Salle to Onondaga, the capital of the powerful Iroquois confederacy, now in New York state. There Robert invited the Indian leaders to a great meeting with the French governor. The conference would be held on the shore of Lake Ontario at the point where the St. Lawrence River begins.

A council of Onondaga Indians

On June 3, 1673, Governor Frontenac led an army of four hundred French soldiers and friendly Huron Indians up the St. Lawrence River. This great army traveled in a fleet of one hundred twenty canoes. When the expedition reached Lake Ontario, it must have looked like a powerful military force.

Instead of attacking the Iroquois Indians who had gathered there, however, Frontenac made friends with them. He was so gracious that the warriors hardly cared that he treated them like children. Frontenac began the meeting with a carefully rehearsed speech.

"Children!" he said, "Mohawks, Oneidas, Onondagas, Cayugas, and Senecas. I am glad to see you here, where I have had a fire lighted for you to smoke by, and for me to talk to you. You have done well, my children, to obey the command of your Father. Take courage: you will hear his word, which is full of peace and tenderness. For do not think that I have come for war. My mind is full of peace, and she walks by my side. Courage, then, children, and take rest."

Governor Frontenac brought many gifts and distributed them freely. The Indians were greatly impressed, both by Frontenac's powerful army and by his kindness. A formal peace treaty was agreed upon. The agreement not only called for peaceful relations between the Indians and the French but also allowed the French to build a fort along the Lake Ontario shore. The soldiers began erecting Fort Frontenac immediately.

The French expedition returned to Montreal in triumph. Not a single man, not even a single canoe, had been lost.

A painting of three Indians of the Iroquois confederacy. The warrior in the middle wears a British coat, probably symbolizing the British-Iroquois alliance of the 1700s.

Father Jacques Marquette

French explorer Louis Jolliet

Back in Montreal, Frontenac and La Salle began to discuss the details of Robert's plans. They agreed that he would set out to explore and fortify the Mississippi River with French troops. Both men also agreed that it would be best for Robert to travel to Europe first. There, he could meet with King Louis or one of his aides and get approval for the first stages of his operation. But before La Salle left, astonishing news arrived.

In 1674, the fur trader Louis Jolliet returned to the St. Lawrence from travels in the west. Two years earlier, he had led a small party of French explorers in a search for the upper Mississippi River. With him was the Jesuit missionary Jacques Marquette. Their venture was a complete success.

The great river, at last, had been found. Jolliet and the others had traveled down the Mississippi for much of its length, going as far as the Arkansas River. Making careful measurements and drawing maps along the way, Jolliet was certain that the Mississippi flowed into the Gulf of Mexico. Although his records from the trip were lost in a canoeing accident, he reconstructed them as soon as he returned home. One of his maps showed the Ohio River and included the words, "the river discovered by the Sieur de La Salle."

Jolliet and Marquette had fulfilled La Salle's own dream of finding and exploring the Mississippi River. Now Robert was even more determined to set up a French empire along the Mississippi. In his vision, it would stretch from the Great Lakes all the way down to the Gulf of Mexico. It would cover vast, unexplored lands to the west and reach to the Appalachian Mountains in the east.

Marquette and Jolliet entering the upper Mississippi River

La Salle set sail for France in 1674. Upon his arrival, he lost little time traveling to the palace of Versailles. This was the lavish home of King Louis XIV and the five thousand people in his court. The crude buildings of Montreal must have seemed shabby compared to the magnificent palace. There, amidst flowing fountains, formal gardens, and marble hallways, the people in Louis's court wore powdered white wigs and expensive perfumes. Their talk was full of the latest rumors, the latest scandals, and the moods of the king and his aides.

Robert La Salle had little interest in the gossip whispered in the halls of Versailles. Instead, he presented court officials with letters from Governor Frontenac, describing La Salle in glowing terms. He stayed at Versailles during the winter of 1674 to 1675. During

The palace at Versailles

that time, he met King Louis XIV and developed an important friendship with the king's top aide, Jean Baptiste Colbert. Besides being France's finance minister, Colbert was in charge of naval affairs. It was his job to carry out the policies of the king of France on the high seas and in France's overseas colonies, including New France.

Through this powerful friend, La Salle received help from King Louis himself. By order of the king, he was declared a nobleman and became a member of the French aristocracy. Although noblemen were usually given titles, such as count or baron, La Salle was not. He already had a noble-sounding phrase as part of his name: the Sieur de La Salle. Now the gentleman from La Salle had become the nobleman from La Salle.

Above: Louis XIV, king of France
Below: Jean-Baptiste Colbert

Robert La Salle petitions King Louis XIV.

With Minister Colbert's assistance, Robert was made governor of Fort Frontenac, the small French outpost built on the shore of Lake Ontario. La Salle agreed to pay France back for the expenses of building the fort. From his own fur-trading profits, he would pay the soldiers stationed there, and he would also encourage settlers to move nearby.

In the spring of 1675, La Salle hurried back to Canada. There, he gave Governor Frontenac the good news of his success at the French court. Then he immediately traveled up the St. Lawrence River to take command of the little fort.

Fort Frontenac was deep in the Canadian wilderness. Robert went to work immediately to make it a decent place to live. He had the old fort torn down and constructed a new one, built out of stone. The workers built barracks to house soldiers, a mill to grind wheat and corn into flour, and a bakery. They cleared more than a hundred acres (forty hectares) of forest land to make room for arriving settlers and their farms. Boats, bigger than the largest bark canoes, were built to carry supplies on Lake Ontario.

Before long, Fort Frontenac became the center of the richest fur trade in New France. The reason for its success was simple. The stone fort was built 180 miles (290 kilometers) up the St. Lawrence River from Montreal. Indians no longer had to make the long and difficult trip down the St. Lawrence to trade in Montreal. At Fort Frontenac they could trade their furs for the inexpensive manufactured goods they wanted. Besides, fur-bearing animals along the river were already becoming scarce. But in the Great Lakes region west of Fort Frontenac, they were still plentiful.

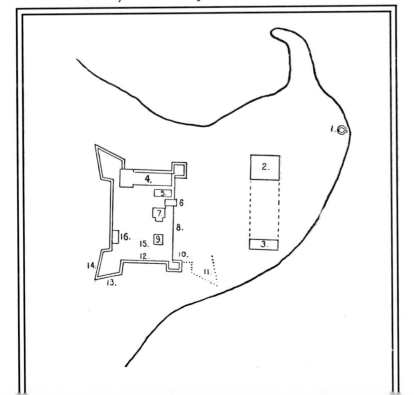

A diagram of Fort Frontenac, built on a peninsula extending into Lake Ontario

Almost from the beginning, many people in Montreal were angered by the success of Fort Frontenac. Fur traders resented losing business to this western settlement. Jesuits were enraged when Robert brought priests from a different religious order to his fort. Soon a number of people decided to act against him.

When supplies for the fort were ordered from Montreal, the shipments were delayed time and time again. Furs sent back to Montreal from the fort were lost or stolen. La Salle's enemies spread false rumors among the Iroquois Indians that La Salle's troops were preparing to attack them. The same people sent letters to King Louis and his ministers accusing La Salle of all kinds of crimes. Some people also tried to create disagreements between Robert and his brother Jean.

La Salle even became the target of a would-be assassin. One day after he had finished eating a meal at the fort, La Salle suddenly became sick. Poison had been placed in his salad by a man named Nicolas Perrot, who worked at Fort Frontenac. Perrot said he poisoned the food to help the Jesuit priests of New France, who felt that La Salle was their enemy.

Robert was gravely ill for more than a month. Many people at the fort thought he would die. But he finally regained his strength and showed that he was a fair and kind man. Although he disliked the Jesuits, he soon made it known that the priests had played no part in the attempted murder. "I clearly discovered the falsity of the accusation which this rascal had made against them [the Jesuits]," he wrote in a letter to a friend in Paris.

For Perrot's crime, La Salle could have had him executed. Instead, he pardoned him. In the same letter, Robert wrote that he did not want the incident to cause embarrassment to the Jesuits.

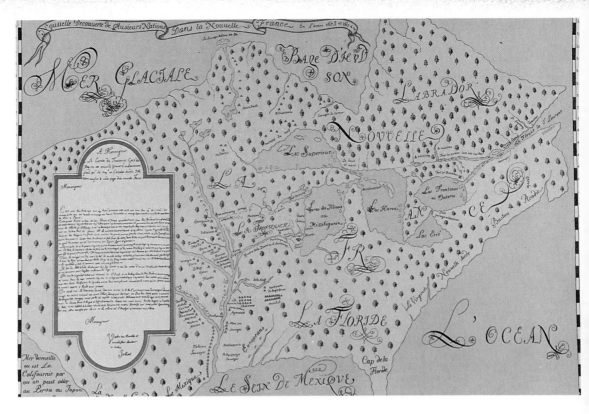

Jolliet's 1674 map of North America

In the fall of 1677, Robert La Salle left Fort Frontenac and traveled by canoe past Montreal to Quebec. There, where the St. Lawrence River widens as it approaches the Atlantic, he boarded a ship for France.

For years, La Salle had dreamed of exploring the land south of the Great Lakes on the great Mississippi River. He had also dreamed of building forts along the river, so that the vast American interior could become part of the French empire. Now he was prepared to share with King Louis and his ministers those full plans.

Officials in King Louis's court had received many letters from Montreal describing La Salle as a madman. Nevertheless, they met La Salle graciously. Many of Robert's friends, both in the New World and in France, had written letters in support of Robert and his exploration plans. One letter described how much better—and warmer—the land was south of New France.

Scene of a settlement in the North American wilderness in the sixteenth century

"It is nearly all so beautiful and so fertile," the letter said, "so free of forests, and so full of meadows, brooks, and rivers; so abounding in fish, game, and venison, that one can find there in plenty, and with little trouble, all that is needed for the support of flourishing colonies. The soil will produce everything that is raised in France. Flocks and herds can be left out at pasture all winter. . . ." The letter went on to describe the crops that could be grown there, adding that the native Indians were friendly and had no modern weapons, since they had not traded with Europeans.

"It was the knowledge of these things," the letter continued, "joined to the poverty of Canada, its dense forests, its barren soil, its harsh climate, and the snow that covers the ground for half the year, that led the Sieur de La Salle to undertake the planting of colonies in these beautiful countries of the West."

Canadians today might be surprised to hear their beautiful country described so harshly. But the letter, and La Salle's visit as well, had one specific purpose. Robert La Salle wanted to convince the king of France to establish forts and colonies along the Mississippi River.

In just a few days, La Salle received his answer in an official document signed by Louis XIV. Permission was granted to explore the great river southward and to set up forts. Those forts could be owned personally by La Salle. The king expressed hope that his subject might find a route to Mexico. La Salle was granted unlimited profits from the trading of buffalo hides, which were far less valuable than beaver skins. As before, however, the expenses of the venture had to be paid by the explorer, not by the king of France.

Louis XIV and officers of his staff

A portrait of French officer Henri de Tonti, showing his artificial right hand

With King Louis's permission to begin his great adventure at last, Robert immediately set out to raise money. He obtained part of the funds from friends and acquaintances in France and even more from members of the large Cavelier family. He expected to repay all the loans, with interest, from profits he would make in the wild American interior.

While La Salle was still in France, he met a handsome young Italian, still in his late twenties, named Henri de Tonti. Tonti had become a citizen of France and had served as an officer in the French army. Robert soon learned that Tonti wanted to explore the New World. But when he first met the young officer, La Salle saw that he had lost his right hand.

Tonti explained that, during a battle, a grenade had exploded in his hand. La Salle wondered how someone so badly wounded could survive in the rugged American wilderness. Tonti had a quick answer. He handled a sword and a pistol in his left hand with great skill, he said. As for his missing hand . . .

Tonti raised his right arm above his head and smashed it against the wall. An iron fist, attached to the end of his arm and concealed by a glove, struck the wall with a sound like a gunshot. This fist had earned the young officer the nickname Iron Hand. Tonti explained that he could defend himself one way or another.

Robert La Salle was convinced. He decided to make Henri de Tonti his top assistant. On July 14, 1678, the Sieur de La Salle, Henri de Tonti, and about thirty other settlers set sail for the New World. La Salle's greatest adventure was about to begin.

French frigate on the high seas

Chapter 6
The Wilderness Traveler

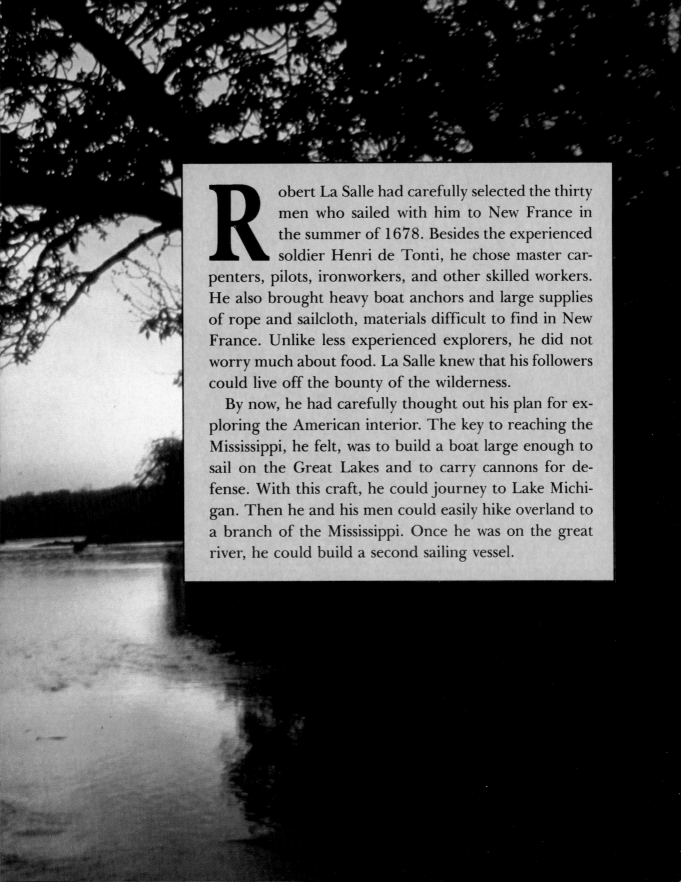

Robert La Salle had carefully selected the thirty men who sailed with him to New France in the summer of 1678. Besides the experienced soldier Henri de Tonti, he chose master carpenters, pilots, ironworkers, and other skilled workers. He also brought heavy boat anchors and large supplies of rope and sailcloth, materials difficult to find in New France. Unlike less experienced explorers, he did not worry much about food. La Salle knew that his followers could live off the bounty of the wilderness.

By now, he had carefully thought out his plan for exploring the American interior. The key to reaching the Mississippi, he felt, was to build a boat large enough to sail on the Great Lakes and to carry cannons for defense. With this craft, he could journey to Lake Michigan. Then he and his men could easily hike overland to a branch of the Mississippi. Once he was on the great river, he could build a second sailing vessel.

There was, he knew, one tremendous obstacle between the St. Lawrence and the western Great Lakes. This was Niagara Falls, the thundering waterfall on the Niagara River between Lake Ontario and Lake Erie. Certainly the falls would destroy any expedition that attempted to cross over them. The men would have to go around the falls, hiking through difficult terrain.

When he arrived in New France during the late summer of 1678, La Salle began preparing for his voyage. In Montreal, he tried to raise more money to buy supplies and materials. At the same time, he sent orders to his assistants at Fort Frontenac. They were told to travel to the Niagara River, to a point just beyond the great falls. There they would build him a sailing ship. To assist them, La Salle sent the master carpenters he had brought from France. In charge of the group was a Frenchman named La Motte de Lussire, who had traveled across the Atlantic with La Salle and Tonti.

La Salle had always tried to have a priest accompany the men working for him. In this case, he arranged for a priest named Louis Hennepin to travel with the carpenters to the Niagara.

In the early autumn of 1678, La Salle and Tonti crossed Lake Ontario to join the workers along the Niagara. The two men had arranged for a second ship to follow them across the lake in a few weeks. This ship would bring to the Niagara site the sailcloth, anchors, rope, and other supplies La Salle had purchased in Europe.

When he reached the Niagara River and made the difficult hike around the falls, La Salle discovered that trouble was brewing. Seneca Indians were watching his men build cabins for the winter. The Indians were suspicious of this "colony" springing up among them.

Louis Hennepin, who explored the Midwest and discovered St. Anthony's Falls, now at Minneapolis. Hennepin wrote several books about his explorations. Though the books were popular, they were full of false claims about discoveries that Hennepin never made.

Niagara Falls

Fortunately, La Salle was by now quite skilled at dealing with Indians. As soon as he arrived, he began passing out gifts and talking with the natives. Before long, their mood had changed to one of friendship.

The next problem, however, proved more serious. News arrived that the supply ship from Montreal had overturned in the Niagara River and sunk. The supplies that Robert had brought all the way from France were lost! Disturbing news came from Montreal as well. People who had loaned money to him were losing faith in his project. Many were demanding that he pay back their investments.

Workmen building the Griffon *alongside the Niagara River*

In February 1679, La Salle and two of his men hiked all the way from the Niagara back to Montreal. On their trek, deep in the cold Canadian winter, they covered 250 miles (403 kilometers). As soon as he arrived at the settlement, La Salle knew he was in serious trouble.

People who had loaned him money now believed his expedition was hopeless. To get their money back, some even seized furs that he had sent back from Fort Frontenac. Others had gone to court, demanding that they be given Fort Frontenac itself. Until then, La Salle had been the legal owner of the fort. The situation was impossible. With what few supplies the men could obtain, La Salle and his followers headed back toward the wilderness. Nobleman or not, the Sieur de La Salle realized that his financial situation was grim.

Despite their leader's difficulties, the workmen along the Niagara River continued building the ship throughout the late winter and spring of 1679. It was finally completed during the summer, while La Salle was battling with his creditors. The ship was named the *Griffon,* after the mythical birds that adorned Governor Frontenac's coat of arms. Soon the ship was moved the short distance down the Niagara to Lake Erie.

On August 7, 1679, La Salle, Tonti, La Motte de Lussire, Father Hennepin, and about thirty others climbed on board the *Griffon* and raised its sails. For the first time, a sailing ship of European design began moving across Lake Erie.

Launching the Griffon

Natural Arch on Mackinac Island

At last, La Salle must have thought, his lifelong dream was coming true. The *Griffon* sailed the length of Lake Erie, about 250 miles (403 kilometers), in just a few days. At the end of the lake was a lovely harbor, not far from the modern city of Detroit, Michigan. The men rested there for a few days and then continued their voyage aboard the *Griffon*. The little ship traveled the full length of Lake Huron. At one point during the voyage, a terrible storm threatened to sink it. After twelve hours of bitter struggle against violent winds and waves, the men were saved when the storm finally died down.

At the northwest end of Lake Huron, the explorers arrived at a rough wilderness settlement named Michilimackinac. During his travels with Jolliet more than five years earlier, Father Jacques Marquette had called the frontier town Mackinac. (A nearby island still bears that name today.) At Mackinac, near the eastern tip of Lake Superior, Lakes Huron and Michigan are joined. Although Mackinac lay deep in the American wilderness, it had become a bustling little community, the center of the fur trade on the Great Lakes.

Here, among the French fur traders, soldiers, Jesuit priests, and Ottawa Indians, La Salle expected to find friends. While he was at Niagara, he had sent ahead fifteen men in canoes to Mackinac. The men were to distribute gifts among the Indians. La Salle hoped this would win their friendship by the time he arrived.

Instead, the advance scouts had ignored their leader's instructions. Most of them traded the gifts for furs and brandy for their own use and then fled into the woods. La Salle discovered that he had no friends at all in Mackinac. Everyone, from Jesuit priests to fur traders, seemed to resent his presence. Bitterly disappointed, La Salle left Tonti behind to try to find deserters.

Aboard the *Griffon,* La Salle and the others sailed on through the narrow channel leading to Lake Michigan. That channel today is called the Strait of Mackinac. By early September, the *Griffon* reached an island on the western shore of Lake Michigan. This island lay near the mouth of Green Bay, an inlet that is now in the state of Wisconsin.

For a time, it seemed as if the expedition's luck had changed for the better. At Green Bay, La Salle found several of the men he had sent ahead from Niagara. The scouts had developed good relations with the Indians who lived nearby. Even more importantly, they had gathered a valuable collection of furs.

A museum exhibit showing the life-style of woodland Indians

La Salle knew that the *Griffon* would not be useful much longer. From the Great Lakes, the men would be traveling south on foot to reach the rivers that flowed into the Mississippi. It would be impossible to carry the ship overland for such a distance. At the same time, he hoped that the furs his men had gathered could be sold to pay his huge debts back in Montreal. So he decided to load the *Griffon* with furs and to send it, with fourteen of his men, back to the Niagara River.

On September 18, 1679, the *Griffon* began the long return voyage. Soon after the ship set sail, La Salle and his remaining men began moving southward on Lake Michigan in four birch-bark canoes. The journey proved difficult. Severe storms on the lake nearly drowned the party several times, and they lost all their supplies, muskets, and gunpowder. Only the hunting skills of a Shawnee Indian scout named Nika prevented La Salle and his men from starving.

Near the southern end of Lake Michigan, La Salle planned to meet Tonti and twenty other men traveling overland from Mackinac. But on November 1, when La Salle and his party arrived at the meeting point, winter was approaching and Tonti was nowhere in sight. While he waited, La Salle built a small fort there, where a river emptied into Lake Michigan. La Salle called it the Miami, and it is known today as the St. Joseph River.

Fort Miami was nearly finished when, on November 20, Tonti and ten others arrived at the St. Joseph River. The new arrivals brought much-needed supplies but disastrous news. The *Griffon*, Tonti reported, had failed to arrive at Mackinac. La Salle must have feared the worst. Could it be that his valuable cargo of furs, needed to pay his debts in Montreal, was lost? His fears were correct. The *Griffon* was never seen again.

On December 3, 1679, La Salle, with thirty-two other explorers in eight canoes, began paddling up the St. Joseph River. They were searching for another river— one that eventually flowed into the Mississippi. That river is now known to be a pair of rivers, the Kankakee and the Illinois. The Shawnee Indian Nika knew exactly where to find the little Kankakee. Unfortunately, Nika was away on a hunting trip when La Salle's party got close to the river.

Present-day scene at the junction of the St. Joseph River and Lake Michigan

Limestone bluffs over the Kankakee River

Tonti and the others paddled their canoes into shore, while La Salle went into the woods searching for the river. Then a sudden snowstorm struck, and La Salle lost his way. By the time he found his way back to the St. Joseph River, it was late at night. He knew his companions would have camped somewhere along the river-bank, but he did not know where. To signal them, La Salle fired a gun. He heard no return shot.

Soon enough, he saw the light of a campfire flickering in the distance. At last, La Salle thought, he had found Tonti and the others. But as he approached the fire, he saw no one sitting by it. A pile of dry grass near the blaze showed that a lone camper had been there recently. La Salle called out in several Indian languages, but there was no answer.

The Frenchman was now too exhausted to travel farther. He added more wood to the dying fire. Next he surrounded himself with a makeshift fence of dry twigs and bushes. If anyone tried to cross the fence, the noise would wake him. Then he went to sleep, warming himself by the fire.

When La Salle awoke in the morning, he saw that the fence may have saved his life. Footprints in the snow encircled it round and round. Clearly, the Indian hunter had returned. Finding no way to get through the twigs and bushes without making noise, he had departed.

In the daylight, La Salle quickly found Tonti and the others. Nika, the Indian scout, had returned to the camp, too. As the men lifted the canoes to carry them on their shoulders, Nika led the way toward the Kankakee River.

The hike was only five miles (about eight kilometers) long. But during the march, La Salle was almost killed. Several of La Salle's French explorers resented his constant pressure to move on, even in the dead of winter. As the explorers walked behind Nika, a Frenchman named Duplessis lifted his loaded gun, pointed it at La Salle's back, and fired!

Fortunately, one of the other men saw what was happening and knocked the gun barrel upward just as Duplessis pulled the trigger. Remarkably, La Salle decided to take no action against the man who had tried to murder him. He felt it best not to upset the other men.

The party soon reached a narrow stream that marked the beginning of the Kankakee River. They put their canoes into the water and loaded in the supplies they had been carrying. After paddling in the sluggish current for just a few hours, they reached a point where the stream widened into a river.

Illinois Indians presenting the peace pipe to French explorers

From here, La Salle's route to the Mississippi River can be traced on any map of the state of Illinois. The Kankakee River flows into the larger Illinois River, which runs directly into the mighty Mississippi. With no mishaps, experienced explorers such as La Salle could have reached the great river in a matter of weeks. Instead, it would be more than two years before La Salle could begin his historic journey down the Mississippi.

At first, the voyage to reach the Father of Waters went well. On January 5, 1680, the explorers arrived at a large village of Illinois Indians. The village lay along the banks of the Illinois River, near present-day Peoria, Illinois. The Indians greeted the Frenchmen cheerfully and fed them well. As a sign of friendship, they rubbed the weary explorers' feet with bear grease. Only a few days later, however, a Miami Indian chief arrived at the village with disturbing news.

The chief told the peaceful Illinois Indians that La Salle and his followers were spies for the Iroquois, who were preparing to attack them. Relations with the Illinois quickly became strained. Fearing bloodshed, six of La Salle's followers, including two master carpenters, crept away in the night.

Undaunted, La Salle did his best to stay on the good side of the Illinois Indians. At the same time, he ordered the building of a new fort, called Fort Crèvecoeur, French for "Fort Heartbreak." He also called for his men to begin building a new ship, one like the *Griffon,* that could sail on the Illinois and Mississippi rivers.

As soon as the fort was built and the new ship started, La Salle decided to split up his followers into three different groups. Father Hennepin and two others were told to paddle down the Illinois to the Mississippi and then to explore the great river.

Tonti was placed in command of Fort Crèvecoeur and most of the men. They would remain at the fort and complete the new ship.

La Salle himself, four other Frenchmen, and Nika would make the most difficult journey. They planned to go all the way back to Fort Frontenac on the shore of Lake Ontario. There they could ask for news of the *Griffon.* They would also be able to stock up on badly needed supplies, especially rope and sailcloth to use in building the new ship.

On March 1, 1680, La Salle and his five companions began the journey back to Lake Ontario. The long trip was full of danger. Just as the Miami chief had warned the Illinois villagers, an army of Iroquois warriors was marching south to attack. La Salle and his men would have to avoid getting caught in the battle. He later described some of the difficulties of the trip.

He wrote that ". . . we must suffer all the time from hunger; sleep on the open ground, and often without food; watch by night and march by day, loaded with baggage, such as blanket, clothing, kettle, hatchet, gun, powder, lead, and skins to make moccasins; sometimes pushing through thickets, sometimes climbing rocks covered with ice and snow, sometimes wading whole days through marshes where the water was waist-deep or even more, at a season when the snow was not entirely melted. . . ."

Along the way, La Salle often set brush fires to cover his tracks so that Iroquois Indians could not follow them. When he finally reached the little fort on the Niagara River, most of his followers were too exhausted to continue. With three fresh men, La Salle hurried on.

Finally, on May 6, he arrived at Fort Frontenac. After sixty-five days of grueling travel in the wilderness, he had covered over a thousand miles (1,613 kilometers). From Fort Frontenac he hurried on to Montreal. There, the money lenders who were fighting over his property were shocked to see him. Within a week, he managed to satisfy his creditors and gather more supplies for his forts, now spread from Montreal to the Illinois country.

Everywhere he stopped along the voyage to Montreal, La Salle was greeted with the bad news about the *Griffon*. The ship, with its valuable load of furs, had vanished. Other canoes, carrying furs he had sent back to New France, had capsized on the rapids of the St. Lawrence River. Most of his property had been taken away. Even worse news awaited him.

La Salle began to retrace his steps to Fort Crèvecoeur by returning first to Fort Frontenac. While he was still there, on July 22, 1680, two French fur traders arrived with a letter from Tonti. Tonti reported that, soon after

French post at Fort Niagara

La Salle had left, the men at Fort Crèvecoeur had deserted, destroying the building and tossing all the supplies they could not carry into the river. Soon it was learned that the deserters had traveled to the little forts at the St. Joseph and the Niagara rivers and had destroyed them. They had also stolen La Salle's supply of furs stored at Mackinac. Now they were on their way to Fort Frontenac to murder La Salle himself.

Such stories of disaster and betrayal surely would have made many men give up. But La Salle was much tougher than that. With nine soldiers from Fort Frontenac, he surprised the Fort Crèvecoeur deserters along the shores of Lake Ontario and arrested most of them. As soon as they were jailed, La Salle organized an expedition to return to the Illinois River. Concerned for Tonti's safety, he hoped to rescue him.

The block house at Fort Mackinac

On August 10, 1680, La Salle and twenty-five men began the long trip back to the Illinois River. At Mackinac and at the fort on the St. Joseph River, he left men and supplies. La Salle was still trying to hold together his string of forts.

Winter had arrived again when the French explorers reached the Illinois River. They could hardly believe their eyes when they saw the Illinois Indians' settlement. The Iroquois had destroyed the village and murdered all the inhabitants. Heads of the dead were perched upon stakes; others were strewn on the ground. Fort Crèvecoeur had been torn down. The half-built ship was in pieces, every nail taken by the Iroquois, who regarded metal as precious. One by one La Salle inspected the severed heads, fearful that Tonti's might be among them. Fortunately, he found no trace of the man.

La Salle searched the countryside for his lost companion, following the Illinois River as far west as the Mississippi. Still unable to find Tonti, he returned to the southern shores of Lake Michigan. At Fort Miami, just east of the modern city of Chicago, La Salle spent the first half of the year 1681 talking with Indians who lived in the area. At the same time, he was recovering from an eye infection, perhaps related to snow-blindness.

While La Salle was at Fort Miami, some of his scouts learned exciting news from Fox Indians camped near Green Bay. Tonti was safe, living with Potawatomie Indians near Mackinac. Eagerly, La Salle paddled a canoe up Lake Michigan to be reunited with Tonti.

From Mackinac the two men traveled back to Montreal, where La Salle met with Governor Frontenac. The Sieur de La Salle and the Count of Frontenac must have discussed the many problems that had plagued La Salle's grand plan to explore the Mississippi and establish forts along the way.

Governor Frontenac understood how La Salle had been betrayed many times by his fellow Frenchmen. Now, La Salle proposed a change in his plan. Instead of leading only Frenchmen, he would invite Abenaki and Mohican Indians to travel with him as well. The expedition was quickly organized. La Salle's collection of French explorers, a priest, and Indian warriors with their wives and children reached Fort Miami on December 21, 1681. By this time, La Salle knew well the fairly easy route to the Mississippi.

At long last, the voyage down the great river was about to begin.

Lac des Assenipoils

99

Chongaskabé ou
Nation des Forts

Missions des
ecollects

les Hanctons

Jadouessans

Lac

A

Buade

Ouïa de Battons ou

Issati

Lac de Condé ou
Superieur

Sault de St
de Padou

R. de S. Fransou

R du tumeau

Mesilimakinac

R. des Bacas
Noire

Lac des Pleur

Ré des Ouisconsin

Baye des Puans

portage

Rt l. Outouaga

Les Illinois

Seignelay

Fort. des M
amis

Colbert

Fort de
Por tage

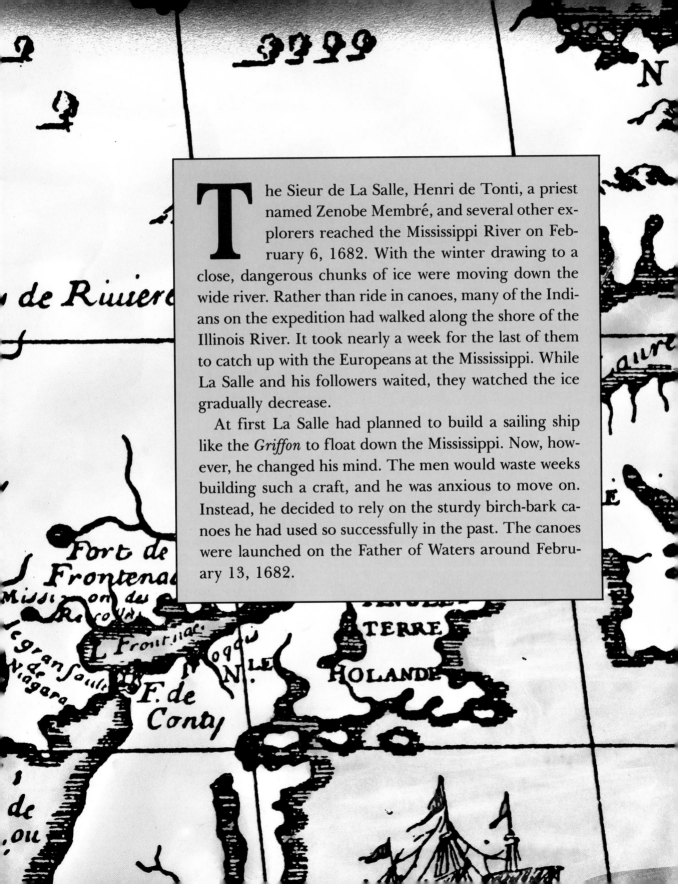

The Sieur de La Salle, Henri de Tonti, a priest named Zenobe Membré, and several other explorers reached the Mississippi River on February 6, 1682. With the winter drawing to a close, dangerous chunks of ice were moving down the wide river. Rather than ride in canoes, many of the Indians on the expedition had walked along the shore of the Illinois River. It took nearly a week for the last of them to catch up with the Europeans at the Mississippi. While La Salle and his followers waited, they watched the ice gradually decrease.

At first La Salle had planned to build a sailing ship like the *Griffon* to float down the Mississippi. Now, however, he changed his mind. The men would waste weeks building such a craft, and he was anxious to move on. Instead, he decided to rely on the sturdy birch-bark canoes he had used so successfully in the past. The canoes were launched on the Father of Waters around February 13, 1682.

Missouri River at sunset

Toward evening on the first day, the explorers passed the mouth of another great river. Emptying into the Mississippi from the west, this river today is called the Missouri. Here at the mouth of the huge Missouri, near the modern city of St. Louis, the width of the Mississippi River nearly doubles. At the time of La Salle's voyage, of course, the area was a wilderness. A few days later, the expedition passed yet another enormous river. This was the Ohio, emptying into the Mississippi River from the east.

La Salle knew he would soon be passing beyond the point that Louis Jolliet had reached ten years earlier.

The explorers would be on a part of the river never before seen by a Frenchman—or, probably, by any European. La Salle also knew that, by the time they reached the Gulf of Mexico, the Spaniards—no friends of the French—might be on the river. He wondered if Spanish soldiers might put an early end to his great adventure.

For the first few days, the explorers saw no one along the banks of the Mississippi. The scattered Indian villages they spotted seemed to be deserted. Had the Indians fled at the sight of the strange expedition?

On February 24, La Salle ordered the canoes ashore near a bluff overlooking the river. There, about midway between the Ohio and Arkansas rivers, the Frenchmen made a camp. Meanwhile, a group of Indians in their party set out to search the countryside for food. Shortly after the hunters left, a Frenchman named Pierre Prudhomme decided to do some exploring by himself.

The Missouri River at its upper reaches in Montana

The Indians eventually returned, but there was no sign of Prudhomme. Some of the hunters reported that they had seen fresh Indian tracks not far from the camp. La Salle worried that his fellow explorer had been killed or captured. While some of the men built a small fort to prepare for a possible attack, others searched for the missing Frenchman.

After six days, Prudhomme finally staggered into camp on his own. Greatly embarrassed, he explained that he had become lost in the thick woods. Delighted at his return, La Salle named the new fortress Fort Prudhomme. He then put Prudhomme in charge of a small group of soldiers he stationed at the fort.

La Salle and his followers had traveled from Canada to the Mississippi River during the coldest part of the year. Now, however, spring was approaching. Compared to the hardships of the past, the long trip down the Father of Waters was smooth and easy. The Mississippi River, although huge, had a gentle current. There were none of the dangerous rapids or frequent obstacles found in rivers such as the St. Lawrence. The river simply flowed on and on, curving lazily through forests and open fields.

On March 13, exactly one month after the voyage began, the explorers neared the mouth of the Arkansas River. This was as far down the Mississippi as Marquette and Jolliet had gone. There the explorers found themselves surrounded by a dense fog that blotted out both shores. Frightening sounds began to reach their ears from the fog-shrouded western bank. They heard the shrill cries of an Indian war dance punctuated by a pounding drum. Robert quickly led his men to the opposite shore.

Fearing an attack, the men rushed to chop down trees

French workmen building a fort

and build a fort. They had been at their work for only an hour or so when the fog lifted. From the opposite shore, the Indians stared in amazement at the strange sight they saw across the wide river. Seeing that the Indians appeared peaceful, some of the Frenchmen waved, urging them to come across.

A small group of the natives, in a canoe made from a hollowed-out tree trunk, paddled halfway out into the river. As usual, La Salle's experience in dealing with Indians saved the day. For just such occasions as this, he carried a calumet. This was a kind of Indian peace pipe, recognized as a sign of friendship by tribes all along the Mississippi River.

Indian peace pipes

He held the calumet high. The Indians, members of the Quapaw tribe, recognized it instantly. When it was clear that relations were good, the explorers paddled their canoes across the river. In a letter written later to his supervisor, the French priest Father Membré described what happened next.

"The whole village came down to the shore to meet us," Membré wrote, "except the women, who had run off. I cannot tell you the civility and kindness we received from these barbarians, who brought us poles to make huts, supplied us with firewood during the three days we were among them, and took turns in feasting us. . . . The young men, though the most alert and spirited we had seen, are nevertheless so modest that not one of them would take the liberty to enter our hut, but all stood quietly at the door."

The Quapaws and the Frenchmen became good friends. The Indians led the Europeans in a festive parade through the neighboring villages. During a religious ceremony in one of the villages, Father Membré gave a long sermon to a large audience of Quapaws. The Indians agreed that it was a fine speech—even though they couldn't understand a word of French!

French traders, called coureurs de bois, *enjoying themselves with friendly Indians in the wilderness*

La Salle proclaiming the French empire in North America

The Indians also failed to understand another part of the same ceremony. With Tonti at his side, La Salle raised a large wooden cross and on it placed the coat of arms of the king of France. He then made a brief speech in French, claiming the land he stood upon for France. The Indians had no way of knowing that the Frenchman was claiming land they believed was their own. After the speech, a volley of gunshots was fired into the air as a festive conclusion to the ceremony.

After three days with the Quapaws, the explorers began heading down the Mississippi once again. This time, two Quapaw Indians came along as guides. With warm spring breezes in the air, the explorers marveled at the beauty of the land. Fragrant meadows, lush pine forests, and haunting cypress swamps came into view as they continued south. The expedition stopped frequently, often visited by friendly Indians living along the banks of the Mississippi. At most of the stops, La Salle repeated the ceremony he had led among the Quapaws, claiming all the land in the area for France. The Indians, of course, had no idea what he was doing.

About 300 miles (480 kilometers) south of the Arkansas River, the Quapaw guides led the explorers to a swampy area on the western bank of the river. Beyond the swamps was a lake, once a part of the Mississippi River, the guides explained. And beyond the lake a huge city could be found. La Salle was intrigued by their description. He sent Tonti, Father Membré, and a few other men in a canoe to look for the city.

After traveling for about two hours, Tonti and Father Membré reached their goal. For Europeans accustomed to the rounded tents and houses of the northern American Indians, the sight was astounding. The buildings of the Taensa Indians, cousins of the Quapaw, were large and almost perfectly square. They were arranged in neat rows, much like houses in a modern city. The walls were built from bricks made of mud and straw and baked. Each house was covered by a domed roof, made from pieces of cane and carefully woven straw.

One of the largest of the brick houses was the home of the Taensa chief. Tonti and Father Membré visited the chief in his home and gave him gifts. The Taensa ruler was so pleased by the visit that he agreed to travel to La Salle's camp to meet the leader of the European expedition. During their meeting, La Salle presented the chief with still more presents. The two leaders parted as friends.

Alligator

Although they may not have known it, the explorers were approaching the southern end of the great river. The air was warm and humid. Some of the animals living in and along the river were much different than those to the north. The Frenchmen were surprised to see dangerous alligators. Several of the monsters were caught and killed for food. Father Membré was surprised to find that the huge alligators were hatched from little eggs, "like chickens."

By the morning after their visit with the Taensa Indians, the explorers were back on the river, continuing the long voyage south. La Salle must have worried that they might soon be spotted by Spanish soldiers. Instead, they saw a dugout canoe filled with Indians. Tonti paddled quickly after it, hoping to meet with the Indians. But as he drew close, an army of a hundred or so warriors, with bows raised, appeared on the shore. La Salle shouted a retreat, and they raced for the opposite shore.

After a simple camp had been made, Tonti and a few others crossed the river in a canoe. Tonti held high the peace pipe, and once again the Indians recognized the sign of peace. Members of the Natchez tribe, these Indians joined hands in friendship. Tonti, having only one hand, asked his fellow explorers to take his place.

La Salle and the others soon crossed the river too, and traveled to the Natchez village. Today, the modern city of Natchez, Mississippi, is located not far from that village. During the visit, La Salle once again planted a cross with the arms of France attached in the middle of the natives' town. Soon afterward, the explorers visited another Indian village a short distance south.

On March 31, 1682, the expedition paddled by the mouth of the Red River, the last of the big rivers flowing into the Mississippi. Three days later, they spotted a group of Indians fishing in dugout canoes near the edge of the river. The Indians fled, but La Salle sent a small party of men after them to investigate. As the men approached the marshy bank, a shower of arrows fell around them. In the long journey down the river, this was the only time La Salle's expedition was attacked. Wisely, the men retreated and joined the others moving quickly down the opposite side of the river.

Three days later, on April 6, 1682, they reached a point where the river divided into three wide channels. La Salle decided to split the expedition into three parts, one to follow each of the channels. He took the westernmost branch, Tonti explored the middle, and a trusted assistant led a group along the eastern branch.

Traveling by canoe down the Mississippi was quite a different experience for La Salle's party than their earlier explorations in large sailing ships.

As La Salle continued down the river, now leading a smaller group of followers, he realized that the ocean was near. The current was extremely slow, and the water was salty, a clear sign that it was mixed with salt water from the Gulf of Mexico. A fresh breeze from the ocean broke through the humid air. Soon, the wide vista of the gulf spread out before him. He had arrived, at last, at the end of a journey he had planned for more than a decade.

For the first time, a European explorer had traveled the great Mississippi River from the north to its end in the broad deltas of the south. Also for the first time, a European had journeyed from the St. Lawrence River to the Gulf of Mexico, through the heart of the North American interior.

Along the swampy borders of the gulf, the three parties quickly found one another and gathered together for a great ceremony. La Salle built a monument on the shore. Father Membré led them in religious hymns.

Finally, La Salle made a great speech, claiming all the land he had crossed, and much more, for the king of France. In honor of King Louis XIV, he named the new land Louisiana. To honor the king's minister, Jean Baptiste Colbert, he named the great river he had just traveled the River Colbert, although the name Mississippi was known to him.

In his speech, La Salle said that he gave to King Louis and the other French kings who would follow him "possession of this country of Louisiana, the seas, harbors, ports, bays, adjacent straits, and all the nations, peoples, provinces, cities, towns, villages, mines, minerals, fisheries, streams, and rivers, within the extent of the said Louisiana, from the mouth of the great river St. Louis, otherwise called the Ohio . . . as also along the river

Bayou near New Orleans

La Salle claiming all the lands drained by Mississippi for the king of France

Colbert, or Mississippi, and the rivers which discharge themselves thereinto, from its source . . . as far as its mouth at the sea, or Gulf of Mexico. . . ."

The Sieur de La Salle had given the king of France a mighty gift. The land that he claimed for France today includes all or parts of the states of Arkansas, Missouri, Iowa, Minnesota, North Dakota, South Dakota, Nebraska, Oklahoma, Kansas, Montana, Wyoming, Colorado, and Louisiana. The ceremony on the marshy shore of the Gulf of Mexico must have marked La Salle's proudest moment.

At the time, however, he had little idea how much trouble and misfortune lay ahead of him.

Chapter 8
End of the Dream

When René-Robert Cavelier, Sieur de La Salle, reached the mouth of the Mississippi River in April 1682, it was still more than half a year before his fortieth birthday. At the time, he could not have known that the last five years of his life would be filled with tragedy and despair. Bad luck struck almost immediately.

Few animals fit for eating could be found on the land around the Mississippi delta. With the expedition's supply of food rapidly diminishing, La Salle decided to head north on the vast river. He planned to retrace his long journey all the way back to Canada.

For a time, the explorers managed to live on alligator meat, but as they continued north, the alligators disappeared. Not far from the Red River, La Salle and his followers reached a Quinipissas Indian village. In exchange for knives, tobacco, and a few axes, the Indians gave the hungry travelers 200 pounds (91 kilograms) of corn. That night, however, they attacked the explorers' campsite. The Frenchmen managed to drive them off with musket fire. At dawn, La Salle and his companions quietly pushed their canoes into the Mississippi River and slipped away.

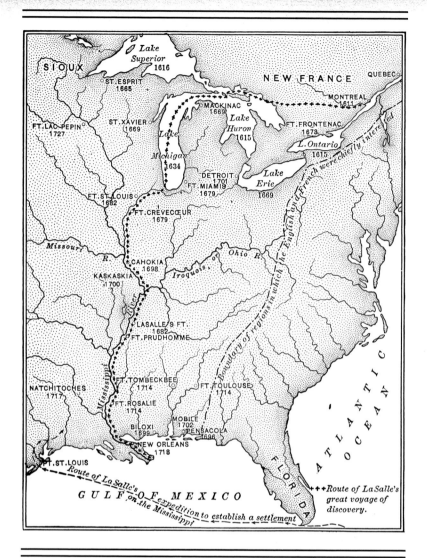

The map shows the following labels:

SIOUX

NEW FRANCE

QUEBEC

Lake Superior 1616

ST. ESPRIT 1665

MONTREAL 1611

MACKINAC 1669

Lake Huron 1615

FT. LAC PEPIN 1727

ST. XAVIER 1669

Lake Michigan 1634

FT. FRONTENAC 1673

L. Ontario 1615

DETROIT 1701

FT. MIAMIS 1679

Lake Erie 1669

FT. ST. LOUIS 1682

FT. CREVECŒUR 1679

Boundary of regions in which the English and French were chiefly interested

Missouri R.

CAHOKIA 1698

Iroquois, or Ohio R.

KASKASKIA 1700

LASALLE'S FT. 1682

FT. PRUDHOMME

Mississippi River

NATCHITOCHES 1717

FT. TOMBECKBEE 1714

FT. TOULOUSE 1714

FT. ROSALIE 1714

MOBILE 1702

BILOXI 1699

PENSACOLA 1696

NEW ORLEANS 1718

FT. ST. LOUIS

FLORIDA

ATLANTIC OCEAN

Route of La Salle's expedition on the Mississippi

GULF OF MEXICO

expedition to establish a settlement

+ + Route of La Salle's great voyage of discovery.

Map of La Salle's explorations

The voyage northward on the great river continued. Although they now had to paddle against the current of the Mississippi, the explorers had an easy journey in their swift birch-bark canoes. Eventually, the expedition reached Fort Prudhomme, which La Salle had built on the way down the river. Just as he arrived at the tiny fort, La Salle fell seriously ill.

"On the way back I was attacked by a deadly disease," La Salle wrote later, "which kept me in danger of my life for forty days, and left me so weak that I could think of nothing for four months after." Father Membré cared for the sick explorer at Fort Prudhomme. Meanwhile, Tonti and a group of others traveled on to Mackinac on the upper Great Lakes. From there, news of the great discovery could be passed on to the governor of New France in Quebec.

Had he heard the latest news from Canada, La Salle might have become even more ill. His friend and supporter, Governor Frontenac, had been driven from office and had returned to France. In his place was a new governor, named Le Febvre de La Barre. La Barre listened closely to the bankers, traders, and priests in Montreal who hated La Salle and opposed his plan to conquer the Mississippi. Soon, La Barre sent soldiers to seize Fort Frontenac, to take La Salle's supply stations at Niagara and Mackinac, and even to capture the little forts La Salle had built along the Illinois River.

By the end of September 1682, La Salle had regained enough strength to return to Mackinac. There, Tonti gave him some of the news from Canada. At the time, neither man knew that La Barre was sending armed troops to take away their forts and storehouses. Although he was still exhausted from sickness and the long voyage, La Salle decided to move quickly to strengthen his position on the Illinois River.

He told Tonti to gather as many men as possible and travel south to the Illinois River. He was to return to the spot where Fort Crèvecoeur (Fort Heartbreak) had been built and then destroyed in 1680. La Salle hoped to establish a colony of Frenchmen and Indians there. The settlement would include a storehouse for furs and a fort to protect the area from the Iroquois. When he learned that the Iroquois were indeed on the warpath, La Salle quickly followed Tonti to the Illinois River.

*View of the Illinois River from
Starved Rock State Park*

Not far from the old site of Fort Crèvecoeur was a towering stone bluff. The huge rock rose about 125 feet (38 meters) above the land around it, with three sides as steep as castle walls. On top, overlooking the Illinois River valley, the rock was broad and flat. Just two years earlier, in the valley below, peaceful Illinois Indians had been cruelly massacred by invading Iroquois. For the moment, at least, the Iroquois were gone. More than six thousand Indians, all more or less friendly to the French, had returned to the valley. The great rock overlooking the Illinois River valley was a perfect place, La Salle and Tonti decided, to build a new fort.

By the spring of 1683, the men had completed the fort at the top of the immense rock. La Salle named the new fortress Fort St. Louis. Today the fort is gone, but the great rock remains. Named Starved Rock in later years, the massive bluff overlooking the Illinois River near Chicago is a popular tourist spot.

Even before Fort St. Louis was completed, La Salle began to notice that supplies he had ordered from posts on the St. Lawrence River were delayed again and again. He soon learned that Governor La Barre had arrested several of his men who had gone to Quebec to buy more supplies. Finally, a messenger from the St. Lawrence brought news of La Barre's plans to destroy all of La Salle's settlements.

The explorer now realized that the highest government official in New France was trying to ruin him. There was only one thing La Salle could do: cross the Atlantic once again to enlist the aid of King Louis XIV.

He lost little time. With Nika, the Shawnee Indian scout, La Salle crossed the ocean in the fall of 1683. By November he was back in France. So was his brother, Jean. By chance, Jean Cavelier had decided to visit his family and friends in Europe at the same time Robert was hurrying to visit King Louis.

In a matter of days, the Sieur de La Salle was speaking directly to the French king. Louis had received dozens of letters from Governor La Barre and others in Canada describing La Salle as selfish and unpatriotic. But the king understood the explorer better than his enemies in Canada did.

Louis sent a stinging letter to La Barre, demanding that all of La Salle's forts and supplies be returned immediately. He let it be known that he and his advisers had even bigger plans for the French in the New World.

A 1758 map of the Mississippi River delta as it was conceived at the time

Before the great voyage down the Mississippi, French government officials had thought that Spanish soldiers completely controlled the land around the Gulf of Mexico. Yet La Salle had not found a single Spaniard anywhere near the mouth of the great river. This surprising news gave the king and his advisers an idea.

Why not establish a French colony at the mouth of the Mississippi? This way, the French could control the river and the entire American interior through which it flowed. Maybe they could even take control of the Gulf of Mexico from the Spanish.

La Salle agreed with the king. On July 24, 1684, a fleet of four ships set sail from France for the Gulf of Mexico. On board were La Salle, his brother Jean Cavelier, his nephew Moranget, Nika, a hundred French soldiers, and many laborers, skilled tradesmen, shop-keepers, even young women and children. Chickens, pigs, goats, and cows were brought along as well, so that livestock could be bred in the new colony.

Unfortunately, many of the men aboard the ships were thieves, pirates, and other shady characters. One witness described the soldiers as "mere wretched beggars . . . many too deformed and unable to fire a musket." About the laborers, the witness said, "the selection was so bad that when . . . they were set to work, it was seen that they knew nothing at all."

The voyage across the Atlantic proved to be a complete disaster. As soon as it began, the *Joly,* the largest of the four ships, had to return to port for repairs. This forced the other ships to turn back as well. When the voyage resumed, La Salle and the fleet commander, Captain Beaujeu, began to argue furiously.

Over the years, La Salle had grown accustomed to total authority over his followers. But by order of King Louis, Beaujeu was placed in command of the voyage until they reached the New World. He and La Salle argued constantly. The arguments so weakened La Salle that he became seriously ill once again.

By the time the fleet reached the Caribbean islands, just off the continent of North America, La Salle was delirious with fever. Worse yet, Spanish pirates captured the fleet's supply ship, along with all the food, tools, ammunition, and building supplies. Making matters even worse, Spanish colonial officials had found out about French plans to settle at the mouth of the Mississippi.

Santo Domingo

As Robert La Salle regained his strength and his senses, he became aware of where he was. He and the remaining three ships were docked at the city of Santo Domingo on the island of Hispaniola. Santo Domingo is the oldest European colony in the New World, founded by the brother of Christopher Columbus.

The explorer quickly realized that his plans were falling apart. His supply ship was gone. Many of the French soldiers and future colonists who had sailed with him were wandering about the streets of Santo Domingo. Some were already infected with local diseases that they would carry to the new colony. Several were killed in barroom brawls. Many others had deserted.

La Salle knew that the voyage had to be completed before all was lost. He was forced to spend two months in Santo Domingo recovering his health. But by late November he was strong enough to come aboard ship. Immediately, the three remaining ships set sail for the northern shore of the Gulf of Mexico.

It was a dangerous voyage. Spanish warships were patrolling the waters all around the southern coast of North America. Luckily, the French ships managed to slip through Spanish patrols in the Gulf of Mexico.

On December 28, 1684, five months after the fleet left France, the expedition caught sight of the mainland along the gulf. At this point, La Salle made the first of several tragic mistakes that eventually cost him his life.

In his historic voyage down the Mississippi, the explorer mistakenly thought that the river was much closer to Mexico than it actually is. Using the best maps available to him, he decided that the river's mouth must be to the west of his present position. Following his instructions, Beaujeu began steering westward.

The captain and the explorer continued arguing. Beaujeu, fearing the dangerous rocks and shoals near the mainland, refused to lead the ships near land. It was difficult to make out any details along the coast. But the details hardly mattered, for the little fleet of ships was already west of the Mississippi. Each day the expedition sailed on, they left the river farther behind.

Gradually, La Salle began to realize that his ships were sailing in the wrong direction. On January 6, 1685, he decided to go no farther. At this point the fleet was actually more than 400 miles (640 kilometers) west of the Mississippi. Supplies on the ships were dwindling, many of the passengers were sick with fever, and the fights with Captain Beaujeu were growing worse.

In desperation, La Salle made another tragic decision. He decided to lead all his followers ashore and then march eastward to find the Mississippi. On January 20, the soldiers, explorers, and colonists climbed into lifeboats and rowed toward the shore. The spot where they landed is now called Matagorda Bay. It is in the state of Texas, about midway between the cities of Houston and Corpus Christi.

From the start, the landing was a disaster. A group of settlers wandered into a band of local Indians and immediately began to squabble. La Salle and a squad of soldiers left the beach to settle the dispute. While the leader was gone, one of the ships, holding most of the expedition's remaining supplies, ran aground and was torn apart in the pounding surf. Nearly all of the ship's tools, weapons, food, and medicines were lost.

La Salle asked Captain Beaujeu to steer the *Joly* eastward and to return after finding the Mississippi. Beaujeu seemed willing to follow La Salle's request. The *Joly* indeed sailed away . . . but to France, never to return.

Throughout the next two years, the settlers tried to live in the barren landscape of the gulf coast. For a while, they lived fairly well on the local game, seafood, and fruits. The settlers had brought seeds from France, but in the hot, salty air, the crops soon withered and died. The livestock brought from France did little better. Many of the colonists became deathly ill. Others died of rattlesnake bites or poisonous plants. Then the last of the ships from France, the little *Belle*, ran aground and was destroyed while exploring the coast. The settlers were now completely stranded.

By the start of 1687, most of the pitiful settlers had died or had wandered away into the wilderness. Of the

Thicket of pines

150 settlers who had landed at Matagorda Bay two years earlier, only about forty remained.

Facing the increasing hatred of some of his followers, La Salle made a desperate plan. He gathered twenty of the strongest men and boys remaining in his colony, including his brother Jean, his nephew Moranget, and Nika. The men, he decided, would hike east, find the Mississippi, and head up it until they found Tonti and his soldiers. La Salle had left Tonti with orders to build up the fortresses along the Mississippi. Now he hoped his assistant could help to rescue the other colonists.

The men began their desperate journey on January 7, 1687. The weather was often stormy, and game along the way was scarce. They trudged across plains, through forests, and into swamps with water up to their knees.

A hunting party in the wilderness

On March 15, they camped near the Trinity River in what is now east Texas. They still had not found the Mississippi, and their food was almost gone.

La Salle sent out a hunting party led by Nika, and they managed to kill two buffalo. When he sent his nephew Moranget to help bring back the buffalo, Moranget got into a quarrel with the other hunters. That night, the hunters murdered Moranget, Nika, and another man in their sleep.

By the morning of March 18, 1687, the hunters still had not returned. La Salle, worried about Moranget, decided to walk to their camp to investigate. The murderers had already decided to commit yet another murder to cover up their crimes. As La Salle approached the camp, they hid in some high reeds. When their leader was practically on top of them, they fired. A bullet struck him in the head, and René-Robert Cavelier, Sieur de La Salle, died instantly. He was forty-three years old.

The assassination of La Salle

With La Salle's death, his dream of building a French colony on the Gulf of Mexico also died. Soon after, the assassins got into an argument with each other, and two were killed. The others fled into the wilderness. Seven men and boys who remained loyal to La Salle, including Jean Cavelier, managed to reach the Mississippi. There they eventually found La Salle's faithful friend Tonti, busy organizing affairs at Fort Prudhomme. Tonti listened to the terrible news and then helped the men return to France.

The French settlers who stayed behind on the coast along the Gulf of Mexico were not so fortunate. The few who did not die from disease or battles were captured by Indians and carried away to an unknown fate.

The vast area of America that La Salle claimed for King Louis XIV remained in French hands for nearly a century. It was acquired by Spain in 1763 and returned to France by a secret treaty in 1800. In 1803, under the leadership of President Thomas Jefferson, the United States purchased the land, called Louisiana, from the

Map showing the Louisiana Purchase and other territories acquired by the United States from 1783 to 1867

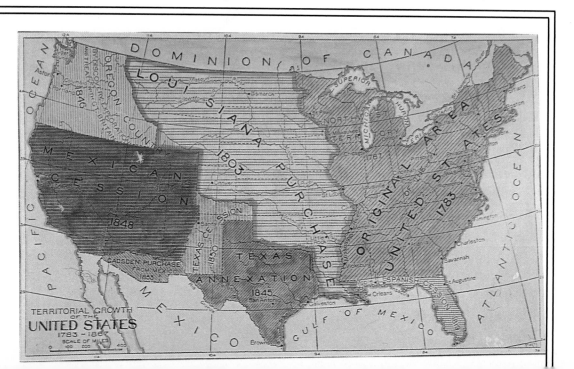

French government for about $15 million. In one stroke, Jefferson more than doubled the size of the United States.

Even today, La Salle's influence can still be seen along some of the great rivers of America's heartland. The city of La Salle, Illinois, along the Illinois River not far from Starved Rock, is named in his honor. From the little Kankakee River, to the Illinois, and on down the mighty Mississippi, a few cities and towns still bear French names and still boast of residents descended from French settlers.

René-Robert Cavelier, Sieur de La Salle, hoped to establish a French empire in America. He did not quite succeed. Yet after more than three hundred years, many reminders of his brave deeds still remain.

Above: A portrait of La Salle. Below: United States president Thomas Jefferson, who approved the Louisiana Purchase

Appendices

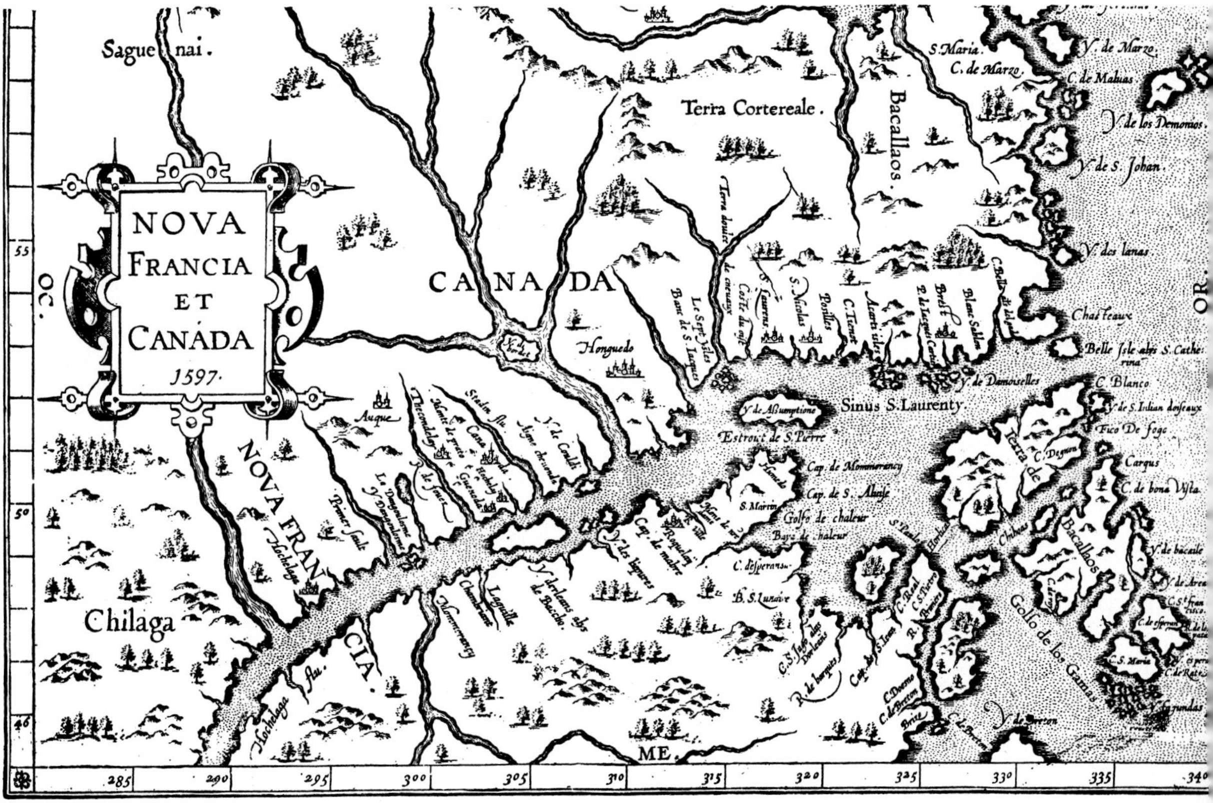
NOVA FRANCIA ET CANADA 1597.
Sague nai.
CANADA
NOVA FRANCIA
Chilaga
Terra Cortereale.
Bacallaos.
Sinus S. Laurenty
Hongedo
Golfo de los Gamas
ME.
OC.
OR.

Above: A map of New France and Canada made in 1597, forty-six years before La Salle was born. In 1535 French explorer Jacques Cartier became the first European to discover the St. Lawrence River, the major waterway of New France.

Opposite page: In this stunning photograph of the earth taken from a space shuttle, the mighty Mississippi River—known to Algonquin Indians as the Father of Waters—can be seen snaking its way down the North American continent.

In 1682, La Salle landed in an area inhabited by the Natchez Indians, once the most powerful tribe in the lower Mississippi region. Natchez, Mississippi, was named after the tribe. The city became the endpoint for the Natchez Trace, an important supply route in the 1800s. The area shown above was once a hideout for pirates and thieves who preyed upon travelers in the region.

Magnificent Niagara Falls, the waterfall on the Niagara
River between Lake Ontario and Lake Erie.

Timeline of Events in La Salle's Lifetime

1643—René-Robert Cavelier, Sieur de La Salle, is born in Rouen, France; Dutch mariner Abel Tasman explores the South Pacific Ocean; Swedes make first permanent settlement in what is now Pennsylvania

1644—In China, the Manchus conquer all of China, replacing the Ming dynasty with the Ch'ing dynasty

1647—Massachusetts colony establishes first public school system in the colonies; Rhode Island is chartered as a colony

1648—The Peace of Westphalia ends the Thirty Years' War, Europe's religious conflict

1649—British king Charles I is executed and the Parliament assumes power; Maryland colony passes North America's first religious toleration law

1650—Dutch colonists settle Africa's Cape of Good Hope

1652—The Dutch establish Cape Town, South Africa

1660—Charles II becomes king of England and restores the monarchy

1661—French king Louis XIV begins his reign

1664—British capture New Netherlands from the Dutch, renaming it New York; the French East India Company is founded

1665—The plague kills over 68,000 in London

1666—La Salle first arrives in Canada; a great fire sweeps through London

1669—La Salle begins his first exploration up the St. Lawrence River

1670—Charleston, South Carolina is founded

1672—Boston Post Road is completed between Boston and New York City

1673—Louis Jolliet and Jacques Marquette explore the Mississippi River

1678—Louis XIV grants La Salle permission to set up forts and explore the Mississippi Valley

1680—Scientist Isaac Newton explains gravitational attraction of the sun, moon, and earth; in Pueblo Revolt, Indians of America's Southwest drive out Spanish conquerors; New Hampshire is chartered as a colony

1681—William Penn receives a land grant for most of what is now the state of Pennsylvania

1682—La Salle explores the Mississippi River all the way to the Gulf of Mexico

1683—Battle of Vienna ends the Muslims' threat to Europe; Taiwan becomes part of China

1684—La Salle leaves France to establish a French colony at the mouth of the Mississippi River

1685—Edict of Nantes, protecting religious liberties of French Huguenots, is revoked

1687—La Salle is murdered by members of his expedition party; Venetians bombard Turks in Athens, Greece, badly damaging the Parthenon; Isaac Newton publishes his *Principia mathematica*

Glossary of Terms

allowance—A sum of money for expenses

altar—A table-like stand for religious ceremonies

ammunition—Bullets or other explosive objects fired from guns

anonymous—Not named or identified

assassin—A murderer

capsize—To turn over, as a boat in water

cobblestone—A rounded stone used to pave streets

colonial—Having to do with a colony, or settlement, of people

colonists—People from one country living in a new territory

confederacy—A group of peoples who join together for one purpose, such as protection or trade

conference—A meeting

continent—One of the seven great masses of land on the earth

current—The direction and force of the flow of a body of water

delicacy—A fine food that is rare or very pleasing to eat

delta—Area at the mouth of a river where rich soil is deposited and streams sometimes branch out

deserter—A person who runs away from a military or naval job

diesel-powered—Running by a diesel engine, one that operates by compressing air that causes fuel to ignite and move a piston

estate—A person's land, buildings, and other property

execution—Putting to death as a penalty for wrongdoing

expedition—A trip taken for a special purpose, such as finding something

falsity—Untruth

fisheries—The fish and other water animals in a certain location

fortune—Wealth in terms of material goods

grueling—Difficult; strenuous

heartland—The interior of a state, country, or continent

hectare—A measure of land area, equal to about 2.5 acres

ice-bound—Covered with ice (as a river) so that travel is not possible

inherit—To receive something from an ancestor by legal rights

inlet—A bay or a narrow water passage into or between two bodies of land

investigate—To examine or make inquiries

kilometer—A measure of distance, equal to about three-fifths of a mile

league—Any of various measures of distance, from about 2.4 to 4.6 miles (3.9 to 7.4 kilometers)

makeshift—Crude; put together for temporary use

marsh—Soft, wet land, often covered with tall grasses or reeds

minister—A religious official or preacher

monument—A marker put up to honor a person, event, or location

musket—A large-caliber firearm

plague—A severe, widespread, contagious disease caused by a bacterium

priest—A minister who performs religious rites

rapids—Part of a river where the current is swift

resin—A gummy secretion of pine trees

rival—A person trying to reach the same goal as another

scout—A person who searches for a trail or for information

stationed—Assigned to work at a certain location

strait—A narrow strip of water between two larger bodies of water

suicide mission—A task that is likely to be unsuccessful or even to cause death

trek—A difficult or complicated journey

Bibliography

For further reading, see:

Cox, Isaac J., ed. *The Journeys of Rene Robert Cavelier.* 2 vols. NY: AMS Press. Reprint of 1922 edition.

Jacobs, William Jay. *Robert Cavelier de La Salle.* NY: Franklin Watts, 1975.

Joutel, Henri. *Joutel's Journal of la Salle's Last Voyage.* NY: Burt Franklin. Reprint of original edition.

Le Clercq, Chretien. *First Establishment of the Faith in New France.* 2 vols. NY: AMS Press, 1973. Reprint of 1881 edition.

Osler, Edmund B. *La Salle.* NY: Longman, 1967.

Parkman, Francis. *La Salle and the Discovery of the Great West.* Williamstown, MA: Corner House, 1968. Reprint of 1889 edition.

Weddle, Robert S. *Wilderness Manhunt: The Spanish Search for La Salle.* Austin: University of Texas Press, 1973.

Index

Page numbers in boldface type indicate illustrations.

Picture Identifications for Chapter Opening Spreads

6-7—View of the Mississippi River from Riverview Park, Hannibal, Missouri

14-15—A drawing of Rouen, France, by J. M. W. Turner

28-29—Detail of a 1670 Flemish map of North America

38-39—Sunset and ice patterns on the frozen backwaters along the Illinois River

50-51—The treacherous Lachine Rapids of the St. Lawrence River

68-69—The Kankakee River at Bourbonnais, Illinois

86-87—Map of eastern North America, from Louis Hennepin's 1683 *Description de la Louisiane*

100-101—The mighty Mississippi near Muscatine, Iowa

Acknowledgment

For a critical reading of the manuscript, our thanks to John Parker, Ph.D., Curator, James Ford Bell Library, University of Minneapolis, Minneapolis, Minnesota

Picture Acknowledgments

©REINHARD BRUCKER: 104

©VIRGINIA GRIMES: 74

H. ARMSTRONG ROBERTS: 11, 119

HISTORICAL PICTURES SERVICE, CHICAGO: 4, 8, 12, 17, 20, 21, 22 (2 photos), 23, 27, 31, 37, 49, 52, 54, 56 (top), 57, 59 (2 photos), 60, 63, 66, 70, 72, 73, 80, 92, 94, 99, 114

NORTH WIND PICTURE ARCHIVES: 2, 10, 13, 14–15, 16, 18, 19, 24, 25, 26, 28–29, 34, 40, 41, 43, 44, 47, 56 (bottom), 58, 61, 64, 65, 67, 71, 86–87, 93, 102, 106, 108, 112, 113, 115 (2 photos), 117

©ROB OUTLAW: 89, 111

PHOTRI: 9, 30 (2 photos), 55, 83, 91, 97, 116, 118

R/C PHOTO AGENCY: ©RICHARD L. CAPPS, 75, 84; ©JEANNE HALAMA, 77

©JAMES P. ROWAN: 6–7, 32, 45, 68–69, 78

SHOSTAL ASSOCIATES/SUPERSTOCK INTERNATIONAL, INC.: ©ERIC CARLE, 100–101

TOM STACK & ASSOCIATES: ©BOB SELL, 88; ©WENDY SHATTIL, ROBERT ROZINSKI, 96

TONY STONE WORLDWIDE/CLICK-CHICAGO: ©WILLARD CLAY, 5, 38–39; ©DON SMETZER, 98

VALAN: ©KENNON COOKE, 50–51

COVER ILLUSTRATIONS BY STEVEN GASTON DOBSON

About the Author

Jim Hargrove has worked as a writer and editor for more than 10 years. After serving as an editorial director for three Chicago area publishers, he began a career as an independent writer, preparing a series of books for children. He has contributed to works by nearly 20 different publishers. Some of his Childrens Press titles are *Mark Twain: The Story of Samuel Clemens, Gateway to Freedom: The Story of the Statue of Liberty and Ellis Island, The Story of the Black Hawk War,* and *Microcomputers at Work.* With his wife and teenage daughter, he lives in a small Illinois town near the Wisconsin border.